CASEY EUGE

G000075103

INVISIBLE
OUTSIDER

From battling bullies to building bridges,
my life as a Third Culture Kid

Summertime
Publishing

First Published in Great Britain in 2022 by Summertime Publishing

ISBN: 978-1-915264-01-5

Edited by Joshua Parfitt (www.joshuajames.xyz)

DISCLAIMER
This memoir is a truthful recollection of actual events in the author's life. Some conversations have been recreated and/or supplemented. The names and details of some individuals have been changed to respect their privacy.

ACKNOWLEDGMENTS

... to my mother, Tena, without whose personal life choices, inspirational wisdom and unconditional love, this myriad of memories would not have been possible

... to my loving wife, Yuki, whose undying patience, understanding, and support of this project, while simultaneously working on her dissertation, makes me forever indebted

... to my two fathers, Tom (my biological dad) and Wade (my stepdad), whose extraordinary strength, devotion, and perseverance taught me never to give up on my dreams

... to the countless teachers and professors who have gifted me with knowledge and understanding throughout my schooling

... to the many international students who have shaped my world and friendships

... to Ruth Van Reken, who first taught me the term 'TCK' and whose life, work, and legacy have encouraged TCKs around the world

... to Joshua Parfitt, my editor, who sliced and diced my words with the culinary skills of a master chef and to whom I owe the deepest debt of gratitude

... to all those who cry out against racial injustice and strive for the unity of humankind

CONTENTS

FOREWORD

In early 19th-century England, David Brewster designed and patented the first kaleidoscope, describing his invention as capable of creating an "infinity of patterns." One hundred and fifty years later, I spent hours of my childhood staring through the eyepiece of a descendant of Brewster's design. My kaleidoscope probably cost a dollar. It was made of plastic and filled with cheap colored beads.

It didn't matter.

Inside that tube, magic abounded. Colors danced, lurched, split, in ways that were both erratic and perfectly coherent. No matter what happened, no matter which scrap of plastic knocked into which mirror, it all made sense inside the kaleidoscope.

Psychologists use the term "coherence" to describe when something makes sense, particularly the way somebody is able to speak about their life. "Coherence," Erik Hesse once wrote, "is the hallmark of mental health." Not everybody achieves coherence in their lives. Some can't discern a pattern. Some give up. Some feel their beads have spilled all over the floor. For many, coherence remains a distant, unreachable island, like Hawaii.

What you have before you is a carefully crafted kaleidoscope. It is an act of coherence. It is the synthesis of a life. Casey Bales has taken the shards of his cultural misfittings and blended them into a dancing, lurching, and ultimately coherent whole. Casey faced so many erasures of his identity, restarts to his personality, and misunderstandings of his background that his beads could have spilled all over the floor. He could have lost his way. Oftentimes—like all of us—he felt like he had.

But he stayed with it. Shard by shard, piece by piece, he gathered the cultural fragments of his life into a tube, and he carried on. Many times—like all of us—he must have felt like quitting. But he persevered.

The result is a story of cultural courage. This book, fundamentally, is an *act* of courage. If we had told Casey as a twelve-year-old that he would one day write a book about his life in English, he would have laughed and told us we must be mistaken—in Japanese. This book is a statement to all who doubt that the collection of one's experience leads to the production of something unique and inspiring.

The students whose lives Casey now touches are, in fact, the beneficiaries of a life well-synthesized, a life where all the pain of not having belonged has been transmuted into the ability to make others feel belonging. This alchemy has become Casey's calling. This book is his bugle.

May this book stand as a lighthouse to all who feel lost on their cultural way. Inside *Invisible Outsider*, colors and pieces that don't seem to belong are wrought into harmony. Casey's is a message for our times, spoken quietly and from the shores of his own experience. But his is also a message for all times:

for all of us, the quest for a coherent life means finding how every experience fits, however sharp and jagged.

May you enjoy the view, and may it spur all of us to achieve and maintain our own sense of coherence and purpose.[1]

Drs. Douglas W. Ota
Psychologist, Researcher, Author & Presenter:
www.safepassage.nl
Author of S*afe Passage: How Mobility Affects People and What International Schools Should Do About It*
Founder, Safe Passage Across Networks
(SPAN): www.spanschools.org

---

[1] A fitting visual tribute to this Foreword's metaphor for Casey's book can be found here: https://www.youtube.com/watch?v=gxxqdrrpgZc

CULTURE
JAPANESE
STUDENT
AMERICAN
BILINGUAL
WORLD
FIRST
TCK
NEW
CULTURE SHOCK
EXPERIENCE
DIFFERENT
DIVERSITY
ENGLISH
LIFE
HOME
LEARN
PEOPLE
LIVE
FRIENDS
INVISIBLE OUTSIDER
LANGUAGE
THIRD CULTURE KID
TOLERANCE
ISLAND LIFE
THROUGHOUT
BECOMING
TWO
HAWAI'I
ESL
INDIANA
FEEL
BEING
UNIVERSITY
HIGH SCHOOL
FAMILY
WORK
TOKYO
COUNTRY
THE WAY
PLACE
TIME
GROUP
STUDY
ABROAD
TRAVEL
VISIT
FOREIGN
COLLEGE
TEACHER
IDENTITY
EMPATHY
TRADITION
ARRIVAL
ACCEPTANCE
PLAY
FELT
TEXT
BALANCE
STAGES
ENTRY
DEPARTURE
EDUCATION
ASIAN
BOY
SAME
HELP
PARENTS
HAVING
AGE 3
REMEMBER
UNDERSTANDING
FIND

PREFACE

If you travel to a new country or immerse yourself in a new culture, you're likely to experience the phenomenon of culture shock. There's a lot of debate about how exactly it works, but many agree that culture shock can be summarized into five stages. These five stages (see below) are the foundation of both my academic work and the outline of this book. Though they don't know it, many people from many walks of life get stuck at Stage 2 as they can't – or won't – adjust and adapt to new cultures. For me, growing up between Japan and America and having to adapt for my survival and wellbeing has gifted me the tools to find my place in the world as an adult Third Culture Kid (TCK) – and it's these tools I believe the world so desperately needs.

Culture Shock

Before tackling culture shock, let's begin by attempting to define culture. Culture can be understood as the ideas, ways of life, values, beliefs, arts, and customs of a group of people that are passed down from generation to generation. Though abstract, culture is something that unites and guides a group of people.

Like an iceberg, there are surface parts of a culture that are easy to see, and deep parts that require time to understand and absorb.

The phenomenon of culture shock is a 'psychological disorientation' people experience when interacting with an environment radically unfamiliar to their own.[1] Culture shock does not have to mean moving from one country to another, but could be as simple as joining a new group of people. Fundamentally, it is a basic misunderstanding between people from two different cultures.

Although studies describe the stages differently, there's consensus that culture shock is a stage-based developmental process. The intensity of each stage and the effects on an individual vary from person to person.

While there are mixed opinions regarding the stages, they can generally be summarized into the five stages outlined below. These are based on a 2017 study by American cultural anthropologist Brandie Yale; however, I have modified the stages a little in my book based on my own experience.[2]

1. Honeymoon
2. Culture Shock
3. Adjustment
4. Adaptation
5. Reverse Culture Shock

Symptoms of Culture Shock

According to Simon Fraser University in British Columbia, students embarking on international exchanges or programs should be prepared to experience the symptoms of culture shock, which can differ in their impacts.[3] Some of these symptoms might include:

- Boredom
- Withdrawal (e.g., spending excessive amounts of time reading, avoiding contact with host nationals)
- Feeling isolated or helpless
- Sleeping a lot or tiring easily
- Irritation over delays and other minor frustrations
- Suffering from body pains and aches
- Longing to be back home
- Unduly criticizing local customs or ways of doing things

STAGE 1: HONEYMOON

The honeymoon stage can be viewed as an exciting time. The foreign world you are experiencing is fascinating and new. You are eager to find similarities with your own culture and pay little attention to differences, turning a blind eye to aspects that are annoying. This is an enjoyable time, which can last from a few days to a few months. During this period, you are exploring the food, places, and customs of the new environment. As for me, I did not have a honeymoon stage when I initially moved to Japan as I was only three years old.

STAGE 2: CULTURE SHOCK

Culture shock begins when the initial excitement wears off. The differences between the culture you are familiar with and the new culture become more apparent, leading to irritation and frustration. Language barriers may occur, and customs might appear old and outdated or not make any sense. As a reaction, you might start to withdraw from situations and feel emotionally vulnerable. In the worst-case scenario, you may develop prejudices against the host culture and think of the people and their customs in a negative way.

STAGE 3: ADJUSTMENT

In the adjustment stage, things will start to get better. Gradually, you begin to accept the differences and change your thinking accordingly. Even though you might prefer the ways of your home culture, you will begin to develop an increasing open-mindedness toward the host culture. As you learn the language and/or customs and get into a routine, you will relax more. You will stop overthinking or questioning *why?* and simply accept how things are done. There will still be difficulties, but you'll be able to handle them.

STAGE 4: ADAPTATION

In the adaptation stage, you'll feel very comfortable and at ease with the host country. This stage usually comes after 18 months. Here, you should be able to communicate with strangers easily and not feel as isolated as before. Your new culture feels familiar and you're comfortable accepting cultural differences. Taking part in social interactions with locals may become a frequent occurrence, and there may even be occasions where you become critical of aspects of your home culture. Most importantly, you achieve a sense of belonging and feel as if this is your new home.

STAGE 5: REVERSE CULTURE SHOCK
The last stage, sometimes called re-entry shock, can evoke the same feelings as culture shock. When returning to your home culture, you may experience depression or sadness because friends and family do not share the same enthusiasm regarding your cross-cultural experience. If you were away for an extended period of time, you may encounter feelings of frustration or irritation from members of your home community because your new cultural values and mannerisms clash with theirs. In many cases, you may feel like you don't belong in your home community anymore. After a while, you will readapt to your home culture while retaining a newfound perspective of the world.

NOTES

1   Oberg, K. (1960). Cultural shock: Adjustment to new cultural environments. *Practical Anthropology*, (4), 177-182.
     https://doi.org/10.1177/009182966000700405

2   Yale, B. (2017). Understanding culture shock in international students. *Academic Advising Today*, 40(4). Retrieved from:
     https://nacada.ksu.edu/Resources/Academic-Advising-Today/View-Articles/Understanding-Culture-Shock-in-International-Students.aspx

3   International Student Advising and Programs. (n.d.). Stages and symptoms of culture shock. Simon Fraser University. https://www.sfu.ca/students/isap/explore/culture/stages-symptoms-culture-shock.html

LIVING AMID PANDEMIC RACISM (2020-2021)

A Global Pandemic

"How many times have we gone on this twilight date?" I asked my Japanese wife of three years as we picked up the pace of our sneakers on our daily walk. It was a ritualistic outing we'd resigned ourselves to since the advent of COVID-19. Wearing matching Hawaiian Crazy Shirts (Hawai'i's largest shirt-printing facility) along with our government-mandated face masks, we let the trade winds grant us our moment of escape.

"Hmmm... I couldn't count the times we've marched downhill to the end of the road!" she answered. "Maybe it's because I'm with you, but I never tire of seeing the same beautiful ocean view." She sidestepped the tropical grass bursting through the concrete crevices as if she were dancing, and I placed my arm around her waist to steady her. I didn't want her to fall. Behind those steady, brown eyes, I knew she was dealing with the pandemic in her own way.

I was proud of her, but afraid for her. I knew the Donald Trump-endorsed label for COVID-19 – the 'China virus' – had slanted the national mood against people like her. I'd seen from the news how Asian and Pacific Islanders were being targeted by Americans for the irks and pains caused by the pandemic, to the point of threats and assault. I felt tense. And relieved to be living in Hawai'i where the Aloha Spirit cultivates more acceptance toward racial differences.

I'd been planning to take Yuki to Indiana to meet members of my extended family who were unable to attend our wedding in Hawai'i back in 2018. However, anti-Asian sentiment was much worse on the mainland. I was hesitant to travel, not only for our health, but also for our safety.

I grew up seeing masks in Japanese schools whenever someone just had a runny nose or cough. It made sense. *Why are there so many Americans who can't see the logic of such a simple gesture?* I thought. In the far distance, Honolulu city lights twinkled like urban stars ready to wish upon.

Just then, a neighborhood cat, who we'd named *Ten-chan*, greeted us as we made our way home along the wide concrete sidewalk. We'd given her that name because she was a magnificent attention seeker, hence the abbreviated -*ten* from *attention*. The suffix *chan* is a Japanese honorific commonly used for girls or cute pets.

We headed inside our two-bedroom ground-floor town-house to rustle up an evening meal. Not surprisingly, Ten-chan followed us over the doorstep hoping for a tasty treat.

It's funny we gave her a Japanese rather than an English name (Yuki grew up in Los Angeles and speaks better English than I do Japanese). I was reminded momentarily how kindness and community spirit were values instilled in me growing up in Japan – values currently under attack in the age of a global pandemic. And that's not just through anti-Asian racism; when citizens verbally abuse each other over mask-wearing and conspiracy theories, it's the values of cohesion and togetherness in society in general that are under attack. Ironically, very Confucian, very Chinese, values. None of the anti-Asian prejudice was against *me*, an average white American on the outside, but it was like my instincts ran counter to my nation's. I felt under attack, too.

Hate Crimes

According to news reports, the new coronavirus originated from China, either from a wet market or a laboratory.[1] Unfortunately, negative political rhetoric about China incited old tropes about Asian people and ignited a slew of hate crimes. There was a rise in accounts of Asian Americans and international visitors being ostracized, harassed, and discriminated against. On May 20, 2020, *USA Today* announced that "people of Asian descent have reported being shunned, verbally abused, name-called, coughed and spat on, even physically assaulted as the coronavirus pandemic continues to upend American life."[2] In fact, there were over 2,000 hate crime incidents in the United States throughout 2020, a 150% increase on 2019.[3]

I found this troubling, despite my marriage to a Japanese

woman, because many of these attacks were directed toward Chinese, Japanese, Thai, Korean, Malaysian, and other Asian cultural groups at random. I was familiar with this type of behavior from the early 2000s, when anti-Arab sentiment ripped through the country in the wake of the September 11 attacks. One of my Muslim classmates at the International School of Indiana said her father – a doctor – had a brick covered in hate speech thrown through his clinic's window. He wasn't even from the Middle East. These disgraceful actions speak of ignorance, violence, white supremacy, and racial discrimination, which promote disharmony within society.

Not since the 1800s had the United States experienced domestic terrorism like the events of January 6, 2021, when a mob of protesters carrying Confederate flags stormed the U.S. Capitol Building and desecrated the hallmarks of American democracy. The protesters had been inspired by the false claims of then President Donald Trump that the 2020 presidential election had been "stolen."[4] The representative hate groups who came forth emboldening white supremacy proved that the ever-present evil of racism was alive and well in our modern age.

Intercultural understanding, on the other hand, enriches both the mind and society as a whole. It gave me hope to see the diversity of youthful masses who protested in the Black Lives Matter movement, a blend of America's multiracial, multicultural, LGBTQIA+ society. I felt energized that change might be on the horizon. And a strange realization hit me: I wasn't proud to be an American citizen; I was proud to be a world citizen. When you navigate wildly different cultures at a young age, you lose that bond to a nation and become bonded to the wider human race. You look at the world perplexed that so much prejudice exists.

Work from Home

In mid-March 2020 I was told to work from home by my employer, Hawaii Tokai International College (HTIC), a small American liberal arts college located in rural Kapolei, Hawai'i, on the island of O'ahu. I was in charge of International Programs, and student exchange groups were cancelled or postponed one-by-one as the coronavirus began to spread from country to country.

Lucky to still be employed, I'd been holed up in my apartment's office, a second bedroom turned into a kind of media center. My wife and I rented the apartment in Makakilo, Hawai'i, just after our marriage. Located high on a hill overlooking the towns of Kapolei and Ewa Beach on O'ahu's leeward side, on most days we could clearly see the distant metropolitan state capital of Honolulu jutting out from the south tip of the island.

Looking back, it was poignant how I derived instinctual pandemic survival techniques from the Asian role models in my life – more so than from their American counterparts. My most treasured Asian mentor, apart from my wife, has been my stepdad, Wade. Half-Japanese, half-Okinawan, and a Japanese *sansei*[5] with Hawaiian cultural roots, he has been a key figure in my life in teaching me a strong work ethic and traditional Japanese philosophy. With a rugged build and heavily Hawaiian, tanned skin, he naturally cuts an impressive character. Aware of this power – and of his *samurai* ancestry – he could cut a person's spirit with a slice of his wicked tongue. It's rare to see him smile. Yet his inner, knowing confidence commands respect all the same.

Growing up, I was fascinated by Wade's dedication to *monozukuri*, or craftsmanship. I spent hours watching him troubleshoot and repair cars, electrical equipment, plumbing problems, and computers. Instead of buying me a brand-new bike, he custom built me one from old bicycle parts. I remember him always saying: "If you borrow something from someone, always return it in a better condition than when you got it." He sees value in old things others just consider junk.

If it hadn't been for those baking hot summers helping Wade lay down topsoil, there's no way I'd have had the energy to create my own little lockdown herb garden. I had lettuce, basil, rosemary, mint, Chinese parsley, chives, and other edibles like arugula and green onion. I'd often chop up *negi* [green onion] for Japanese miso soup or to garnish tofu, adding taste and color. Indeed, Wade's passion for crafting and cultivating – with patience and discipline – spiced up our lockdown dishes no end.

Ten-chan often sat outside in that tiny oasis, unfailing in bringing my attention back from the worldwide pandemic and growing racial animosity. The tranquil setting and gentle greenery helped maintain calm and create a comfortable and inviting shelter to study and work from home, one where Yuki and I could overcome the growing divorce statistics during the COVID-19 pandemic. Although I'd only been married for a few years, I knew that the secret to surviving 24/7 isolation with your partner was having patience, tolerance, and a passion for a hobby. Wade's guidance never failed to prove useful, whether it was garnishing cold tofu or triumphing in holy matrimony.

Duo Projects

The story of my life has been eclectic, which is probably what influenced the project for my Master of Education graduate thesis in Learning Design and Technology. I wanted to prepare American university students planning to study abroad in Japan for the phenomenon of culture shock.[6] My thesis explored how a 3D virtual simulation, developed using Minecraft, might be used to strengthen a student's study abroad experience. It was based on the idea that virtual experiences can be used to immerse students in a target culture so they can learn more meaningfully about the five stages of culture shock.

I know it's unusual for someone as young as me, 35, to write one's life story without some near-death experience or having an album go platinum. Nevertheless, my academic work, combined with the fateful events of 2020, which turned the world upside down and inside out, prompted self-reflection and were a catalyst for reliving moments of the past.

I have been lucky in both my academic and professional lives to watch students go through culture shock and come out of it so much wiser about intercultural conflicts in an increasingly globalized world. This book, both subliminally and actively, is a cross-cultural simulation of my own experience as a TCK, as you join me in real-time through all the culture shock stages. I want to share the journey that many

'Third Culture Kids' (TCKs) walk, because now more than ever the world needs to live under one RULE: Respect, Understanding, Listening, and Empathy. I hope that reading this book will show you what the world we live in could be like.

I have been navigating cross-cultural boundaries ever since I was pulled from Indiana to Tokyo, Japan, at age three. Later, after returning from Japan as a mid-teen, a front-page headline in The Indianapolis Star wouldn't let me forget it: "Mixed blessings for third-culture kids" is how it told everyone about my culture shock in reverse.[7] It's thanks to these early experiences, however, that I passionately believe exposure to unfamiliar places and faces expands perspectives and enriches society. I believe that having a chance to travel, live, or study abroad is critical to expanding a person's worldview and to shifting cultural bias. Cross-cultural experience promotes global literacy, harmony, and mutual understanding. Although the world seems increasingly homogenized, I believe there is unlimited knowledge to be discovered and unknown wonders to amaze the mind.

The essence of this book surprises me, someone who's lived through it, as much as it continues to inspire my work. How I wish I could tell a younger me that travel and culture shock would be my birth pains leading to a lifetime passion for developing tolerance, celebrating diversity, and manifesting acceptance toward all cultures. At last, I understand that having so little in common with my peers was the push to make me realize how much I have in common with people the whole world over.

NOTES

1   BBC Monitoring, & UGC Newsgathering. (2020, January 30). *China Coronavirus: Misinformation spreads online about origin and scale*. BBC. https://www.bbc.com/news/blogs-trending-51271037

2   Phillips, K. (2020, May 20). '*We just want to be safe*': *Hate crimes, harassment of Asian Americans rise amid coronavirus pandemic*. USA TODAY. https://www.usatoday.com/story/news/politics/2020/05/20 /coronavirus-hate-crimes-against-asian-americans-continue-rise/5212123002/

3   Yam., K. (2021, March 9). *Anti-Asian hate crimes increased by nearly 150% in 2020, mostly in N.Y. and L.A., new report says*. NBC NEWS. https://www.nbcnews.com/news/asian-america/anti-asian-hate-crimes-increased-nearly-150-2020-mostly-n-n1260264

4   Guardian staff and agencies. (2021, May 24). *Most Republicans still believe 2020 election was stolen from Trump – poll*. The Guardian. https://www.theguardian.com/us-news/2021/may/24/republicans-2020-election-poll-trump-biden

5   *Sansei* refers to 3rd generation Japanese born outside of Japan.

6   MrBearsAcademy. (2020, March 13). A 3D virtual world journey through the 5 stages of culture shock in Minecraft. YouTube.
https://www.youtube.com/watch?v=8b9IOdsebRM

7   Hooper, K. L. (2000, December 11). Mixed blessings for third-culture kids. *The Indianapolis Star*, A1, A8.

CULTURAL SYNOPSIS

CHAPTER ONE
Identifying And Belonging

This chapter covers my entry into this world and my subsequent destiny. It is not associated with any particular culture shock stage (my experience with the stages of culture shock does not follow the order presented in the Preface).

- I was born a 'Hoosier,' the group name associated with those born, raised, or living in the state of Indiana. This is where I unknowingly entered my first culture.

- I was happy growing up in the proud Indiana heartland of the United States, with the hum of the Speedway in the distance, vast shopping malls, and pork tenderloin sandwiches so large you needed two hands to hold them.

- This was my heritage, my sense of family identity – the ideas, beliefs, traditions, and artifacts gifted by previous generations – an individualist culture applauding values of self-aggrandizement, boisterous outdoor BBQ cookouts, and athletic macho chaps in brimmed trucker ball caps, driving large pick-ups.

■ It was on a long Thanksgiving weekend in 1988 that I first met Japanese people, not in Japan, but in Indiana. Two of Mom's ESL students were staying with us back then in Columbus, Indiana. I was curious to notice how they would huddle close together to whisper behind their hands in Japanese when I did something silly.

■ Had it not been for destiny's plan, my understanding of Japanese culture could have ended where it began – in Indiana with those two ESL students. I might have remained veiled and ignorant of the gifts, richness, and complexities of another culture.

■ I would find myself in the land where Grandpa fought the enemies he considered primitive and deprived. Unlike him, I would thrive in a sophisticated and prosperous culture, making friends with the children and grandchildren of his enemies.

IDENTIFYING AND BELONGING (1986-1989)

The Zodiac and Halley's Comet

I believe my calling was written in the stars – as I believe of each human born into this world. I was born a Fire Tiger under the Chinese Zodiac with personality characteristics describing me as passionate, steadfast, and someone with an unusual spirit of adventure who loves to take on challenges. I'm said to be resolute, energetic, optimistic, trustworthy, and someone who never breaks a promise. In the Western Zodiac, I'm a Pisces. Out of all the Pisceans in the Western Zodiac, the Tiger Pisceans are most inclined to travel and see new places.

Challenges presented themselves from day one. I was born with infant cephalohematoma, a birth condition resulting in a cone-shaped head. Mom had labored for 13 hours in her delivery because my head was too large for the birth canal. For about three months, she and Dad worried about my alien-looking misshapen head until the swelling went down and I began to look a bit more normal.

Some might call Pisceans closed off. I've been told that I can be hard to figure out. I credit this to being born in Columbus, Indiana, in the American Midwest, but being raised and educated in Japan – and in Japanese – from the age of three. To those who know me (and who don't know me), I look Caucasian on the outside, but I feel Japanese on the inside. There have been times in my life when I've been called an 'egg': white outside and yellow inside, to use negative, antiquated racial color slang.

I also attribute my fate to Halley's Comet. Throughout history, comets have been associated with imminent disaster or great global change – I like to believe Halley's Comet foretold the latter. In a dazzling display, the comet streaked across the dark February sky just 10 days before I was born, though perhaps not as a sign of my impending birth, but rather of more historically significant events. It was 1986 and only 12 days prior to its appearance, the Challenger Space Shuttle disaster had occurred, and later, on April 26, the worst ever nuclear power plant accident would occur at Chernobyl in the Ukrainian SSR – it still ranks worst compared to the much more recent 2011 Fukushima Daiichi nuclear power plant catastrophe. The year 1986 continued to prove eventful. *Top Gun* was the highest-grossing film; the Chicago Bears won the Super Bowl against the New England Patriots; and, for the first time, Americans celebrated Martin Luther King Jr. Day as a result of 1986 being deemed the International Year of Peace by the United Nations. Perhaps it was this latter event that best foretold my destiny of becoming a bridge between the East and the West. It's either that or the Patriots going on to win a record-breaking six Super Bowl titles.

Indiana – My First Culture

I was born a 'Hoosier,' the group name associated with those born, raised, or living in the state of Indiana. This is where I unknowingly entered my first culture. Legend has it the label comes from a Native American word, *hoosa*, meaning corn; another legend says it came from the simple question 'who's there?' There are many theories. Nonetheless, Indiana literally means *Land of the Indians*, and though soybeans rank high in terms of agricultural production, the state continues to be best known for its cornfields. The Indy 500 track was close enough to my grandparent's home that you could hear the roar of race car motors in late May of each year. Columbus, known for its modernist architecture, is just 45 minutes south of the capital city, Indianapolis. People growing up around me were predominantly white, middle-class, and lived in homogenized neighborhoods. Only Dr Chen, my pediatrician, was different. He wasn't like everyone else. Why did I recognize Dr Chen as being different? Was it just because of his facial features, or the way he talked, or because it was pointed out to me?

My mother's mother, who passed away in 2005, was a loving woman – generous, and accepting of everyone. Unlike my Grandpa Howard, who could utter a racial slur from time to time – he once slipped and used the pejorative J** in conversation with Wade – Grandma Jane knew no prejudice. She'd been a beautician earlier in her life and felt a sense of duty to make society more beautiful, I guess, in whatever capacity she could.[1] Neither of my grandparents had a college education – Grandma Jane didn't even finish high school. However, to their credit, both she and my grandpa raised children who would all obtain graduate degrees. Even after losing a four-year-old child, my Uncle Dale, to a rare illness known as aplastic anemia, my grandparents pulled themselves up, handled their immense grief, and encouraged Mom and her siblings to study hard and further their educational pursuits.

Twice my grandparents were foster parents for disabled children. When Mom was in high school, they also hosted a Chinese foreign exchange student for a year. I remember meeting him and his family in California in 1989, just before we flew to Japan. Looking back, I wonder if he'd somehow been a factor in Mom's decision to study linguistics and develop her interest in crossing cultures – a decision that ultimately changed the course of my life. As a three-year-old, I certainly didn't realize the significance of the occasion.

It was on a long Thanksgiving weekend in 1988 that I first met Japanese people, not in Japan, but in Indiana. Two of Mom's ESL students were staying with us back then in Columbus, Indiana. I was curious to notice how they would huddle close together to whisper behind their hands in Japanese when I did something silly. Their quiet tones were in stark contrast to the resounding voices of family members. We played together and they even cooked me a typical Japanese savory pancake called *okonomiyaki*. *Yaki* means 'grilled' and *konomi* can be loosely translated as 'whatever you like.' I had no inkling I would soon be transported into their culture, ultimately feeling at home in Japan and becoming as familiar with *okonomiyaki* as a Thanksgiving roast turkey. One of these students, Mutsumi, now works for Temple University, Japan Campus, on the grounds of Shōwa Women's University where I later began my formal Japanese schooling.

Had it not been for destiny's plan, my understanding of Japanese culture could have ended where it began – in Indiana with those two ESL students. I might have remained veiled and ignorant of the gifts, richness, and complexities of another culture. As it turned out, Indiana was not so monocultural for me after all.

Tight-Knit Family

Life in Indiana for my first three years was full of love and tender care. I didn't need to go to a daycare or preschool; I was cared for by my mom, dad, and grandparents. Mom would push me in a stroller all over Columbus to the point of wearing out the wheels of that dark-blue Graco carriage. We would stroll to see Dad where he worked as a manager at a local upscale restaurant, stroll to the supermarket, stroll to JCPenny, and stroll to see Dr Chen. Back then, I was also strapped into a child's car seat in the back of Dad's bright red Cherokee Jeep. I often traveled back and forth between my home in Columbus and my grandparent's home in Indianapolis.

Even to this day, I have vivid memories of washing that Jeep on weekends with a bucket of sudsy water and a hose. This was a typical suburban task enjoyed by many Midwest families, but washing the big Cherokee with my dad made me feel like a man – an American man. I was happy growing up in the proud Indiana heartland of the United States, with the hum of the Speedway in the distance, vast shopping malls, and pork tenderloin sandwiches so large you needed two hands to hold them.

Mom is the eldest sibling and only daughter in her family, followed by Uncle Dave, Uncle Dan, and Uncle Tony. I grew up playing with Uncle Dave's and Uncle Dan's children. My cousins – Adam, Christina, Elizabeth, Terry Joe, John, and Lori – were my tight-knit family cluster. I would always include my cousins in stories I had to write for school. In an action-filled adventure I titled *Ninja*, I saved the planet from destruction with a green-skinned alien ninja by defeating an evil conqueror. In my child's mind, I asked myself in the story: *What would my cousins do?* I felt responsible for protecting them at all costs from anything outside our idyllic community.

Most of my memories, however, are not so out-of-this-world. They're centered around Grandma and Grandpa's antique oak kitchen table, their family room, and the huge green lawn, or family picnics at Uncle Dave's park-like property in rural Batesville, Indiana. When I was at my grandparent's home, I would often play with my Uncle Tony's old set of Matchbox miniature cars and trucks. I loved running in the backyard alongside Fonzie, my uncle's loving, sleek brown dachshund. Uncle Tony, my mom's youngest brother, is a high school advanced placement (AP) calculus instructor and National Consultant for The College Board and Texas Instruments.

One night while dining at a local restaurant, I sat next to Uncle Tony because I had some questions about my math homework that I wanted to ask him. I didn't have a notebook, so Uncle Tony made light work of the restaurant's paper napkins. Later, while waiting for dessert, he tried a trick on the whole table by taking a fork and knife and arranging them into odd configurations. He asked what number between 1 and 10 it represented, while all along he was just illustrating those numbers with his fingers on the edge of the table. He fooled all of us. Uncle Tony bought me my first graphing calculator (a Texas Instruments TI-83) when I entered high school, and along with it, gave me a lifelong love of science.

Grandpa Howard

I may have lived in foreign cultures and eaten many strange things, but not one has convinced me to enjoy zucchini. I hate it. My Grandpa Howard, who was raised on a farm, had been awarded the Healthiest Boy in Marion County, Indiana, distinction in 1941. He was always encouraging me to eat vegetables, and generally I did eat anything put before me on a plate or in a bowl. He was aware of my disdain for all types of squash, but I think he would be disappointed today looking down from above to learn that, as an adult, I never developed a liking for what the Brits call courgette.

He was a disabled veteran, a stalwart Catholic, an avowed Democrat, and a Union advocate living in mainstream Indiana Republican country. My grandfather had already retired after 35 years with Allison Transmission, a division of General Motors, by the time I was born.[2] Grandpa Howard was humble and honorable, both in his life and in his convictions, and his words carried a lot of weight. Talking to him was a serious affair. I would inevitably learn something about health maintenance, history, politics, or current affairs when we were together.

Apart from mowing the grass and maintaining the best lawn in the neighborhood, I remember Grandpa reading newspapers from front to back and watching as many sports competitions on television as he could on any given day – often simultaneously. Back then, I'd sit on his lap and watch the excitement of 'Hoosier Hysteria,' the state basketball championship series, while wearing my bright red Indiana University sweatshirt. Loud cheering could be heard echoing from the house as Grandpa rooted for the home team. There were raised fists and groans of disappointment when they failed to score. I was an American kid. I felt American, and it was natural to be passionate about sports. Grandpa Howard had been a star basketball player during high school, a three-year starter,[3] and had had plans to accept a basketball scholarship to a college in New Mexico until World War II broke out.

I remember a conversation we once had about his military service. I was a boy thrilled with the weaponry and the dangers of war, and I asked him, "Grandpa, what were you most afraid of when you were in the U.S. Coast Guard?"

"Icebergs."

"Whoa!" His response caught me off guard, and Grandpa Howard reeled off stories about all the close calls with gigantic ice monsters in the North Atlantic Arctic Seas – a place known as Iceberg Alley. It was years before I'd see the feature film *Titanic* to properly understand what he was saying.

Grandpa Howard had voluntarily enlisted and served aboard the United States Coast Guard Cutter (USCGC) Southwind, which provided support for allied merchant ships that were en route to the Soviet Union via the Murmansk,

Russia, supply route and engaged in the disruption of German-commanded weather teams stationed in the region.[4] Toward the end of the war, his duty transitioned to the Pacific, where he served aboard the USS Admiral H.T. Mayo naval cargo ship that provided provisions and troop transport through many strategic islands in the South Pacific and on northward to the Japanese mainland. It's ironic that as a soldier, Grandpa first set foot on Japanese soil nearly a half century before me. He saw the Japanese as his enemies; I came to see them as my friends. And as peace activist Floyd Schmoe once stated: "Friends will not make war."[5]

There's another story I will never forget in connection with Grandpa Howard's military service. He once showed me a war souvenir that he kept under the bed in his bedroom. It was an old Japanese bayonet – not a samurai-style sword, but a weapon of great interest to a young boy. Later, after living in Japan, I saw the bayonet again on a visit, still hidden under the bed. It mesmerized me and I snatched it; it became my most prized possession. Later, realizing what I had done, I wanted to return it but was paralyzed with shame. My parents found out and were not happy. They marched me to Grandpa's house where I confessed to my theft, apologized, and returned the bayonet. He was surprised I'd taken it but hadn't even realized it was missing and accepted my apology.

By the age of three, I could nearly recite the full Pledge of Allegiance to my country, America. I was proud to be an Indiana 'Hoosier' and belong to this safe and comfortable community. This was my heritage, my sense of family identity – the ideas, beliefs, traditions, and artifacts gifted by previous generations – an individualist culture applauding values of self-aggrandizement, boisterous outdoor BBQ cookouts, and athletic macho chaps in brimmed trucker ball caps, driving large pick-ups. Although I could have happily remained in Indiana and led the life of a typical American boy, it was not to be. I would find myself in the land where Grandpa fought the enemies he considered primitive and deprived. Unlike him, I would thrive in a sophisticated and prosperous culture, making friends with the children and grandchildren of his enemies.

A Different Destiny

In February 1989, the panda bear I'd been given on my third birthday became my sole companion as I flew from cold and snowy Indiana to Japan – for my mom's new job in Tokyo. She was a teacher of English to speakers of other languages (TESOL) with a master's degree in linguistics and thought some teaching experience abroad would make her more valuable in her chosen career. Her intention was to stay in Japan for only two years; destiny, however, had a different plan that would change my family and me forever.

One month before I arrived in Japan, Emperor Shōwa (昭和)[6], known by his name Hirohito, passed away.[7] Japan was entering the imperial *Heisei* period (平成),[8] meaning *Achieving Peace*, with the reign of Hirohito's son, Akihito. This would be the era of my Japanese experience. I had to write Chinese *kanji*[9] characters like *Heisei* 3 (平成三年) on all of my school papers, instead of writing the year as 1991, for example. My culture shock was just beginning. Later, in 2019, Akihito abdicated the Chrysanthemum Throne, ushering in the imperial reign of his son, Naruhito, who started the current *Reiwa* era (令和),[10] interpreted as *Beautiful Harmony*. More *kanji* for Casey.

Little did I know during my early years in Indiana that I would totally assimilate into the Japanese educational system and earn four diplomas (a complete Japanese education from kindergarten through high school), progressing in each grade as the only non-Japanese student in each class.

I didn't hear the term until I was 14, but I was becoming a textbook definition of a Third Culture Kid (TCK). TCKs are defined as 'people raised in a culture other than their parents' or the culture of the country named on their passport (where they are legally considered native) for a significant part of their early development years.'[11] The term was first coined by researchers John and Ruth Useem in the 1950s, who used it to describe the children of American citizens working and living abroad.[12] TCKs are understood to go on to have different standards of interpersonal behavior, work-related norms and codes of lifestyle, perspectives, and communication. They form a new cultural group that doesn't fall into their home or host culture, but a hybrid culture like all other TCKs. They are generally more tolerant of different cultures and of people from different backgrounds compared to people from the same home country who are not TCKs. In addition, TCKs generally feel better able to adapt to new cultures and understand how to behave in these new environments. Studies indicate that TCKs are more open-minded, hold unprejudiced attitudes toward others, and have diverse cultural values.[13]

I was yanked from the American dream and thrown into a bustling neon-lit concrete metropolis with only Dad, Mom, and a stuffed panda called 'Panda.' My way of life was flipped upside down, with an onslaught of new experiences that came at me like a Tokyo rush hour. Instead of learning to eat my vegetables and potatoes, I was eating *nattō* [a fermented soybean delicacy eaten with rice] and taking my shoes off whenever I went indoors. I bathed with others in large hot pools called *sentōs*, known as public baths in English. To stop me falling onto the subway tracks at bustling stations, my parents harnessed me with a child's leash during those first few months in Tokyo. I hated it.

Reflecting on the past, it's clear how unprepared I was to experience my first taste of culture shock.

NOTES

1   I wanted to mention here that my grandmother attended an inner city interracial high school (Arsenal Technical High School) and later graduated from Madam CJ Walker Beauty School. Madam CJ Walker was the first African-American woman to become a millionaire in the United States.

2   General Motors purchased Allison Transmission in 1929. It was sold in 2007 to the Carlyle Group/Onex Corporation.

3   In basketball terminology, a starter is someone who starts the game on the court, rather than on the bench.

4   The Southwind was instrumental in the 1944 capture of the Nazi naval vessel Externsteine during a skirmish just within the Arctic Circle.

5   Yotsumoto, J. (2018, August 27). *Building houses of peace after the atomic bombs*. NHK World-Japan. https://www3.nhk.or.jp/nhkworld/en/news/backstories/222/

6   The Chinese characters (昭和) translate as follows: (昭) as shining or bright and (和) as harmony or peace.

7   It was during this period that Prime Minister Tojo's political influence and belief in Hitler's philosophy of racial superiority gave rise to his becoming Japan's chief soldier in the events leading to World War II. Hirohito's reign, translated as Bright Peace or Enlightened Harmony, was the longest in Japanese history. The Japan of 1926 had undergone unrecognizable changes by 1989, especially with regard to economic and industrial growth out of post-World War II devastation.

8   The Chinese characters (平成) translate as follows: (平) as even; flat; peace, and (成) as to become; to reach; to attain. The order of Chinese characters depends upon the Japanese meaning and pronunciation.

9   *Kanji* or (漢字) are the Chinese characters used in Japanese writing. I began the perpetual study of *kanji* in 3rd grade. Counting each stroke and precisely outlining the character repeatedly became a daily task both at school and as homework. I was told that a typical high school student in Japan should have a command of 2,000 *kanji* upon graduation.

10   The Chinese characters (令和) translate as follows: (令) as auspicious; order; command; noble, and (和) as harmony; peace. The literal translation of (令) was taken from the

Japanese word *uruwashii* which explained the meaning 'fair' or 'beautiful.' This is the first Japanese era that was named after traditional Japanese poetry rather than classical Chinese literature.

11   Third culture kid. (2021, May 26). In *Wikipedia*. https://en.wikipedia.org/wiki/Third_culture_kid

12   Ruth Hill Useem. (2021, April 27). In *Wikipedia*. https://en.wikipedia.org/wiki/Ruth_Hill_Useem

13   Pollock, D. C., & Van Reken, R. E. (2001). *Third Culture Kids: The experience of growing up among worlds*. Nicholas Brealey Publishing.

QR code for
Chapter One
photographs

CULTURAL SYNOPSIS

CHAPTER TWO
Experiencing Culture Shock 1.0

This chapter is most strongly associated with the second stage of culture shock, commonly known as 'culture shock' or 'entry shock.' This was my first experience of culture shock.

- *Why do I look different?* I wondered.

- *I want to fit in and be like everyone else...* It wasn't so much the physical pain that hurt, but the stress of finding acceptance.

- Rather than being discriminated against as an outsider, in many ways I was privileged to be 'the different one.' In truth, I enjoyed the attention I received every time I was out shopping or dining with my parents.

- Though I was integrating into young Japanese life, these experiences left me feeling trapped in the middle of my identity, not knowing where I belonged.

- I wanted others to recognize that I was the same as them.

■ Cooperation within a Japanese group required structure, uniformity, and a respect for authority. It was important to protect one's face and to reciprocate any greetings, gifts, or favors received.

■ For one of my teachers to take the time to research and find specific Chinese characters appropriate for my name made me very happy. How proud I was to have my name written the same as the rest of the students in my class! It was a rite of passage.

CHAPTER TWO

EXPERIENCING CULTURE SHOCK 1.0 (1989-1995)

Obstacles and Punches

"Mom, I want you to make my hair black. I want to have the same color hair as everyone else. I want to fit in." Earnest and demanding in my tone, I begged Mom to dye my naturally blond hair when I was at elementary school so I'd identify more with my classmates.

"Casey," she replied, "don't you like your blond hair?"

"No!"

"You should be proud of your blond hair," she said. "Your blond hair and blue eyes are part of your identity. You're an American boy."

"But I want to be a Japanese boy." *Why do I look different?* I wondered. *I want to fit in and be like everyone else.*

Before that, I attended a public daycare, Sakurazutsumi, for two years while Mom taught at Asia University in Musashino-shi, Tokyo. It was thanks to our Japanese friends Noriko and Shigeru, who were instrumental in helping me register for the daycare. They acted as our volunteer welcoming committee in those early days of Japanese acculturation and introduced my family to many Japanese foods, festivals, places, and events. Without a doubt, their kindness helped me to flourish in a strange environment. Nearby, in Kichijoji, was my favorite park, Inokashira, full of cherry blossom trees and a big *koi* [1] pond where I loved riding in white, swan-like paddle boats. There was also a children's amusement park with automated rides similar to those at state fairs in the United States. The main difference in the coin-operated rides was that the designs resembled Japanese caricatures and shapes, such as the famous Japanese *shinkansen* ['bullet train'].[2]

Each morning, Dad would strap me in tightly to the back of his *mamachari* bicycle and deliver me to the daycare. A Japanese cultural icon, the *mamachari* is the equivalent of a modern-day horse and cart and comes with a generous seat cushion, a large basket in front, and a place to attach a child seat at the rear. In Tokyo you'll commonly see parents shuttling one or even two children around, hauling groceries, and running errands using this workhorse of a bike. Dad insisted I wear a helmet on my head as a safety precaution in case of an accident. Depending on where you live in Tokyo, riding a bicycle can be a death wish. We were fortunate to live in a less populated area.

It was at the public daycare, I've been told, that I learned my first Japanese word: *unchi*, or 'poop' in English. It may not seem an appropriate first word to learn, but not being able to communicate to the Japanese teacher that you need to potty can have dire consequences. There was a Japanese boy named Yuji I often quarreled with, who, looking back, taught me a few more useful Japanese words to help me survive daycare. I've been told that Yuji bullied me at Sakurazutsumi, probably as a result of my blond hair and lack of language ability. We would occasionally scrap on the school playground, much to the dismay of teachers and staff. It wasn't so much the physical pain that hurt, but the stress of finding acceptance.

Ame to Muchi – Candy and Whip

After two years of Japanese preschool, I was accepted into the co-ed kindergarten that was associated with the prestigious Shōwa Women's University where Mom had accepted a teaching position in 1991. My mom's employment at the university meant I could attend Japanese kindergarten through elementary school for free and, since she wanted to have me in close proximity, we took advantage of that employment benefit.

The kindergarten was a private institution that offered families in the Tokyo area and suburbs a desirable place to send their kids to school. I learned formal Japanese children's writing here, called *hiragana*,[3] and a basic working vocabulary in which to communicate with others. Boys could only attend up until the end of elementary school – to around the age of 12. These types of institutions are common and called 'ladder schools,' where a young girl can begin studies at kindergarten and matriculate into the university after high school. There was a concert hall named after the founding family on campus (the Hitomi Memorial Hall), and it hosted operas, ballet performances, and cultural events we sometimes had to attend. Instead of sitting through boring speeches or church at Catholic school, we sat through tedious cultural performances and couldn't use the restroom unless accompanied by a teacher. We dared not misbehave and cause *meiwaku* – a Japanese word that describes subtle or obvious behaviors and actions that annoy people – for fear of being escorted out, detained, and ridiculed by classmates and parents.

In contrast to the battles against the new culture that would bring tears, there were also joyful moments. The school festival, or *matsuri*,[4] is my favorite memory of Japanese school life. There were parades honoring the Shinto beliefs of a local shrine, and games and Japanese foods at stalls set up on the school property. I loved scooping up the small googly-eyed goldfish with a paper net and taking them home as pets in a plastic bag full of water. I also loved the Japanese soda drink *ramune*. It came in a traditional glass bottle with a marble in the lid you had to push down into the glass with a plunger making a nice 'pop' sound (whether you were a child or an adult).

As well as learning, kindergarten was full of music and song, art projects, plays, and sports. One of my favorite games was rock, paper, scissors – called *jankenpon*. Every day my teacher would play the game with me. Sometimes, I'd play *jankenpon* over and over with my friends. We also used it to decide who'd be the one to clean the toilets during the school cleaning period or to decide who had the first turn at playing some game. My school owned a countryside campus (Shōwa Women's University Tomei Gakurin) that we visited by bus at certain times of the year. We dug sweet potatoes, drank *mikan* juice [a type of Mandarin orange], and hunted small bugs called *dangomushi*. Mom would always find these unfortunate insects curled up in my pockets – a kind of kindergarten currency.

There's a phrase in the Japanese language, *ame to muchi*, that translates literally as 'candy and whip.' While I experienced the 'whip' of the culture, there was also 'candy' that came with it. I enjoyed the attention I received every time I was out shopping or dining with my parents. I was a cute American kid, mischievous, with blue eyes and light blond hair pulled back into a silky ponytail at the nape of my neck. There were several times when people just wanted to feel my hair. Many of the shopkeepers were attractive Japanese girls; I didn't mind *them* touching my hair. Quite often when shopping in a store, I was given a free gift or food from a friendly salesperson. Once I was even given a pair of expensive sunglasses in a department store. Receiving gifts happened so often that my parents were concerned I would become spoiled and learn to expect this celebrity attention! My parents even considered having me return those sunglasses, but instead let that one slide. Rather than being discriminated against as an outsider, in many ways I was privileged to be 'the different one.' In truth, I enjoyed the attention I received every time I was out shopping or dining with my parents. The key was to enjoy the candy and to avoid the whip.

Latchkey Kid

"*Keeshi*," yelled Sho, my first genuine elementary school friend in Japan. He was yelling at me, the blond-headed boy behind him. "*Hayaku*!" [hurry up] he shouted as I ran to catch up with him. "Wanna play video games?"

"Sure, Sho!" I said. "Come over to my place." Sho and I had attended kindergarten together, so he had often visited my place to play games and felt at home there.

We were both carrying heavy black leather backpacks called *randoseru*, a hallmark of elementary school life in Japan. Because we attended a private *shōgakkō* [elementary school] we were required to dress in a military-style uniform consisting of the customary navy blue short pants, white shirt, and navy jacket decorated with pressed gold buttons featuring the school logo, which for us was a cherry blossom. A tasseled navy blue felt hat with a leather bill completed the look. The cherry blossom logo was pinned onto the cap and embossed on the backpack. At the first grade Welcoming Ceremony, then President Kusuo Hitomi gifted each child with a young cherry tree, meant to symbolize our growth and academic achievement. Children were seen as trees that grow dreams. I loved watering that cherry tree on our small outdoor apartment balcony where we lived, even though it was a chore.

Our place was a small 2DK on the eighth floor of an apartment building in the center of Tokyo near Shibuya, in one of the most affluent wards in the city. (A 2DK meant two rooms plus a dining room and a kitchen the size of an American walk-in closet.) The description makes it sound far more spacious than it actually was, but for Tokyo it was an ample space for a family of three. It was located just outside the Shōwa Women's University main gate in a 12-storey apartment building. One room was large enough for two or three children to comfortably sprawl out and play video games, the most popular pastime of young and adolescent Japanese youth. Sho usually stayed for dinner. Solid and big for his age, I was convinced Sho would become a sumo wrestler when he grew up. We shared a love for *Super Mario* and *Donkey Kong* and watched the anime character *Doraemon* on Japanese television.

Tokyo enjoys four seasons, much like Indiana. But my favorite American holidays like Halloween, Easter, Thanksgiving, and Christmas were not recognized in Japan – at least, not in the traditional sense. I do have memories of Halloween and Christmas parties in our tiny apartment with a few classmates. I remember dressing up as a cowboy and bobbing for apples outside our eighth-floor apartment door overlooking the dazzling neon lights of Tokyo. Dad had even bought some pumpkins and showed my classmates how to carve a jack-o'-lantern. But instead of American holidays at home, I became accustomed to collective Japanese celebrations at school or outdoors, like *Setsubun*,[5] *Tanabata*,[6] and *Kodomo no hi*.[7]

I was a latchkey kid. My elementary school was only five minutes away, and I was trusted by my parents to walk home alone, unlock the door, let myself in, and wait for one of them to arrive a short time later. Once, two girls from the university accompanied me back to our apartment. When Mom arrived home a short time later, she got a shock seeing two pretty girls there playing video games with seven-year-old me in the bedroom.

For the most part, the after-school plan worked well until one afternoon when it didn't. I took a detour on my way home from school and visited my favorite video game store. The shopkeeper let me watch an anime film in an adjoining room to the shop, where I lost track of time. When my parents didn't find me home as usual, they freaked out. And understandably so, thinking of a lost American boy in a city of 14 million people. Tokyo police were called. Professors, staff, and students at the university began searching for me. When I was found in the shop an hour or so later, I knew I was in trouble. I forget my punishment, but to remedy the situation, my parents hired a French-speaking Nanny to walk me home from school each day. Although my parents weren't comfortable at first, I guess I was adapting to my new environment. Tokyo felt like a giant playground. I was unaware of the dangers that might be lurking in the shadows. As a latchkey child, I'd lost my freedom, but I'd not lost the excitement for the city.

Pounded into Place

One day while living in that eighth-floor apartment, Mom asked me to carry a plastic bag full of burnable trash down to the garage area on the first floor. Neatly labeled, large plastic bins were located on this floor, and residents were required to separate their burnable, recyclable, glass, and aluminum/steel *gomi* – the Japanese word for trash or rubbish. A volunteer *gomi* monitor was usually present to make sure recyclable items had been properly cleaned and washed before disposal. I was lazy that day, though, and I dropped the bag in the two-foot-wide space between our apartment building and an adjacent furniture store. Mom would never discover my dirty deed, right? But a few days later, she was summoned by no less than the head *sensei* [8] [teacher] of the English Language and Literature Department and asked about it.

I can only imagine the manager of the furniture store had sifted through the bag of trash and found an envelope with Mom's name on it. Since her name was foreign and written in the Japanese script called *katakana*,[9] used to write foreign words, the manager must have suspected she was a professor at the nearby university. To make a long story short, Mom and I had to sincerely apologize to three individuals – the head of her department, the president of the university, and the manager of the furniture store – by deeply bowing and stating in Japanese *sumimasen deshita* and *gomennasai*, or how sorry we were for doing such a thing. I've never forgotten the trouble I caused everyone. It was a life lesson on *meiwaku*.[10]

Unfortunately, the garbage debacle wasn't the only *meiwaku* incident during my early years in Tokyo. Kissing a Japanese girl in my first-grade classroom warranted several phone calls to my parents and a lengthy meeting with school officials and even the girl's parents. Touching or any form of physical contact between individuals is considered poor manners in Japan. Although my parents openly showed affection to me at home, I learned that doing so to others outside the home was inappropriate. In another instance, a few other boys and I were playing in the hall and crashed into a display case containing a large taxidermy of a crab.

Again, there were several meetings with us and our parents, with repeated apologies for destroying the expensive piece of art. In Japan, it's the parents who take primary responsibility for their child's bad behavior.

Although Shōwa Women's University was originally founded on the teachings of the great Russian writer Leo Tolstoy, the moral principles of Confucius formed the underlying foundation of ethical upbringing at Japanese school.[11] Cooperation within a Japanese group required structure, uniformity, and a respect for authority. It was important to protect one's face and to reciprocate any greetings, gifts, or favors received. For example, each elementary student had a task at lunchtimes like preparing and setting out plastic dishware, serving rice, or cleaning up. If I was chosen to serve the rice, my classmates would have to wait in turn to be served. Then, once everyone had been served, our entire table would bow and recite *itadakimasu* before eating. Literally, *itadakimasu* means 'I humbly receive this food' and is also used to thank someone for the meal. Likewise, after eating a meal, we'd say *gochisosama deshita*, which means 'it was quite a feast!' The schools I attended required students to be responsible for *sōji* [cleaning] duties: it was the responsibility of students to participate in cleaning the school building and classrooms. I remember carefully folding *zōkin*, hand-stitched cotton rags, and running the dusting rags up and down, back and forth, across well-worn tiled floors as an assigned task, along with my classmates. This work was not done begrudgingly; we were proud of maintaining our school's image. Plus, we knew we'd get into trouble for doing a poor job. Despite the work, students had fun chatting and making a game out of some of the cleaning duties to pass the time.

It was during my elementary school years in Japan that I learned the meaning of the Japanese proverb *deru kui ha utareru* or 'The nail that sticks up gets pounded into place.' Once, to make friends, I joined a few classmates on our walk home after school. When I tried to lead them in playing a game, I literally got pounded. This sort of taking charge was not acceptable and resulted in me getting into a fight with them. Though I was integrating into young Japanese life, these experiences left me feeling trapped in the middle of my identity, not knowing where I belonged.

My Japanese Name: Keeshi-kun

The scripted words of my blue cardstock birth announcement that my parents had sent to family and friends had proclaimed: 'Casey Eugene, strong, robust and full-bodied, showing finesse and complexity.' My dad, Thomas Bales, a passionate and knowledgeable wine lover, had been a sommelier earlier in his career when he first met my mom. I'm sure those who received that announcement in the mail had a laugh at my entrance into the world being compared to a fine wine. My middle name, Eugene, was given to me by Dad, whose middle name is the same as mine. He and I both got it from my grandfather, a respected dental surgeon in the Indianapolis community who passed away in 1985, shortly before I was born. Together, my name Casey Eugene was meant to convey the meaning 'valorous and well-born.' Later, as a toddler, I was often referred to in rhyme as "Casey Eugene, the Party Machine."

I guess the adults in my life found me somewhat entertaining at that early age – the wine that never ran dry.

Keishi or ケイシー is my name in Japanese writing. Semantically, my name has no meaning in the Japanese language. Thus, when Pokémon characters were introduced, I was fascinated to learn that character #63, known as Abra in English, was named ケーシィ or Keeshi in Japanese. Thereafter, I changed the Japanese spelling of my name from ケイシー to ケーシィ because I thought it was cooler. 'A' is pronounced as a two-vowel combination of 'EI' or 'EE' in Japanese. Because the Japanese language does not have a 'SEE' sound as in my English name, Casey, the closest sound 'SHI' is used to mimic the 'SEE' sound. The *kun* is an informal and affectionate affix added to male names.

In Japan, all non-Japanese people are referred to as *gaikokujin* [foreigner] or *gaijin* [outsider]. Children would often point at me and say *gaijin.* Although it's derogatory in meaning, I became quite accustomed to hearing it and took no offense from it. There were a couple of times, however, that I felt emotionally excluded and verbally bullied. Hearing the following words from a schoolmate hurt me deeply. "You will always be *gaijin,*" he said, insinuating that I would never be accepted in Japan. But I was even more emotionally distraught when a student called me by my last name spelled backwards. My last name, Bales, pronounced 'BE I RU ZU' in Japanese, becomes 'ZU RU I BE' when sounded out backwards. The first three syllables 'ZU RU I' or ずるい is the word for 'unfair' in the Japanese language. To be called 'unfair' in the first grade was a reason to fight. I began to understand from all of these experiences that the Japanese are, generally speaking, cautious of foreigners.[12] Whether the stronger word 'xenophobic' can be used here is debatable, but caution and fear are somewhat connected. Fear breeds discrimination and prejudice in society and, naturally, children learn prejudice from their parents. I believe it's these stereotypes, which children often learn from parents as well as peers, that are the seeds of prejudice and hatred within our communities.

There was another difference related to my name during those early primary years that I was determined to change. It was the writing on my shoe locker. Every child except me had his or her name written in Chinese characters on the front of a wooden locker. My name, however, was written in *katakana*, the writing system used for foreign words. Luckily, a kind-hearted teacher helped me to write my English name Bales into *kanji* [Chinese characters]. It read 米留津 or 'BE I RU ZU.' Basically, the characters represent a phonetic reading of my last name. Collectively, there is no actual meaning; however, each character does represent singular, individual meanings.[13] The teacher also helped me write my first name Casey into 敬士, which does mean something: 'respectful gentleman.' In Japan, your last name is more important and usually comes first, both on paper and in an introduction.

The pictograms that form Chinese writing are usually based on meaning rather than sound. Therefore, it's challenging to write a foreign name in *kanji*. For one of my teachers to take the time to research and find specific Chinese characters appropriate for my name made me very happy. How proud I was to have my name written the same as the rest of the students in my class! It was a rite of passage. Straight away, I began writing my Japanese name on homework assignments, nametags, and anywhere others might see it. I wanted others to recognize that I was the same as them. Because my name was written in the same way as theirs, I was no longer different. I had finally been accepted by Japanese culture and was proud to have a place within the group dynamic. This nail had been pounded into place and, having been accepted, I was determined to avoid further conflict and lead a harmonious life.

NOTES

1   *Koi*, or more appropriately *nishikigoi*, are colorful fish closely associated with Japan's identity and symbolize luck, prosperity, and good fortune.

2   Japan was the first nation to construct a high-speed railway system, beginning with the *Tōkaidō Shinkansen* (515.4 km) in 1964. Throughout the shinkansen's history, there has been a perfect safety record with no injuries or deaths on board. In April 2015, it earned a high-speed world record by achieving a speed of 603 km/h (375 mph).

3   *Hiragana* is one of the three writing systems used in the Japanese language. *Hiragana* is the phonetic alphabet, composed of 46 characters, and is the first writing system Japanese children learn in kindergarten. The alphabet is basically used for particles, words, and parts of words. In Japanese, *hiragana* means 'ordinary' or 'simple.'

4   During a *matsuri*, people worship ancestral spirits and
     certain *kami,* or gods, recognized in the Shinto religion.
     Shinto is the native religion of Japan and is as old as Japan
     itself, associated with the founding of Japan and the reign
     of its emperors. There is a saying that the people of Japan
     are born into the Shinto religion and die as a Buddhist
     – at least within cultural practice and tradition. There are
     millions of *kami*, but only seven deities that are most
     prominent.

5   *Setsubun* is a Japanese lunar festival held on February 2, 3,
     or 4 (a day before the start of spring) and commonly
     involves children throwing roasted soybeans at adults
     wearing *oni* or demon masks. As they throw the beans, they
     shout, *oni ha soto, fuku ha uchi*, meaning 'demons out,
     happiness and good fortune in.' It is also a traditional
     practice to throw roasted beans around one's home, temples,
     and shrines. My first *Setsubun* came as a shock. I was sitting
     in class when my homeroom teacher started passing out
     bags of dried soybeans. Thinking they were snacks, I started
     to eat some when a few teachers wearing *oni* [demon masks]
     suddenly burst through the classroom doors. We then had
     to throw our roasted beans at them and shout, *Oni wa soto!
     Fuku wa uchi!* meaning 'Devils out! Happiness In!' I would
     alternate between throwing a few beans and munching a few
     as 30 kids scrambled to rid the room of the dancing devils.

6   *Tanabata* is known as the 'star festival' and celebrates the
     meeting of two lovers in the Milky Way. Traditionally,
     people write their wishes on strips of colorful paper that are
     tied to bamboo branches. These bamboo branches and
     displays often decorate storefronts and public areas. The
     festival is held on July 7th each year.

7 *Kodomo no hi* can be translated as Children's Day and is held on May 5 each year. On this national holiday, children are honored with special decoration displays and sweet treats.

8 *Sensei* is a formal title used to address a teacher, master, doctor, lawyer, or professional in their field.

9 *Katakana* is one of the three writing systems used in the Japanese language. *Katakana* is specifically used for borrowed and foreign words and consists of 46 characters. It is also used for onomatopoeia. Structurally, *katakana* is an abbreviated or fragmentary form of Chinese writing, called *kanji*.

10 Japan is a group-oriented society where citizens are expected to conform and always be 'all for all.' Being *meiwaku* is bad. There is a popular anime series called *My Hero Academia* where the main hero's ability is called ワン・フォー・オール or 'one for all' and fights his nemesis with the ability オール・フォー・ワン or 'all for one' throughout the story. The hero who possesses the 'one for all' trait fights for everyone, whereas the villain with the trait 'all for one' exudes greed as he absorbs the abilities of others for his own selfish quest for power and domination. This can be a window into how cultural values in Japan clash when there are self-centered people taking advantage of others.

11 According to Geert Hofstede, a Dutch social psychologist and former Professor Emeritus of Organizational Anthropology and International Management at Maastricht University in the Netherlands, the teachings of

Confucius are lessons in practical ethics without a religious content. He writes that Confucianism is not a religion but a set of 'pragmatic rules' for daily life derived from Chinese history. Hofstede presents the following four key principles of Confucian teaching:

> "First, the stability of society is based on unequal status relationships between people. Second, the family is the prototype of all social organizations. A person is not primarily an individual; rather, he or she is a member of a family. Third, virtuous behavior toward others consists of not treating others as one would not like to be treated oneself. In Western philosophy, this is known as the Golden Rule, but without the double not. Confucius prescribes a basic human benevolence toward others, but it does not go as far as the Christian injunction to love one's enemies. Fourth, virtue with regard to one's tasks in life consists of trying to acquire skills and education, working hard, not spending more than necessary, being patient and persevering. Conspicuous consumption is taboo, as is losing one's temper. Everything should be done with moderation."

Hofstede, G., Hofstede, G. J., & Minkov, M. (2010). *Cultures and organizations: Software of the mind* (3rd ed.). McGraw Hill.

12 I have observed that Japanese-American families in Hawai'i may harbor more racist attitudes than Japanese nationals do, at least openly. I suspect this may be due to how unfairly the *nisei* [second generation] of Japanese immigrants were treated following the Pearl Harbor attack.

Many were sent to internment camps on the mainland and in Hawai'i and lost most, if not all, of their personal assets. Extremist views toward *haole* [Hawaiian slang word for white people], *pōpolo* [Hawaiian slang word for black people], and native Polynesians exist as an underlying feeling for some within this group, one that is contrary to the prevailing *aloha* philosophy.

13 For example, (米) can have several meanings depending on the context, such as rice, U.S.A., and meter. (留) is used in several situations and can individually mean to detain, fasten, halt, or stop, but is more commonly used in conjunction with other characters to form words such as (留学) meaning 'study abroad.' Finally, (津) expresses the meanings of haven, port, harbor, and ferry.

QR code for
Chapter Two
photographs

CULTURAL SYNOPSIS

CHAPTER THREE
Experiencing Culture Shock 2.0

This chapter is also associated with the second stage of culture shock. In my case, I experienced this stage twice, once in Japan and once in Hawai'i. Just as I was getting used to Japanese culture by the age of nine, I was abruptly relocated to another environment that was unfamiliar. This was my second experience of culture shock.

- 📖 If six years of living in Tokyo and experiencing that first culture shock at such a young age wasn't enough, I was destined to have another shock.

- 📖 I was a frustrated and confused nine-year-old kid who wasn't used to English as the medium of instruction. I would grumble to my parents and generally felt helpless.

- 📖 "Mom, I hate whoever made English spelling rules!"

- 📖 Although I slowly began to make improvements in my English language acquisition, my cultural understanding had a long way to go.

📖 "Something wrong with your head?" a boy asked. "You stupid, yeah?"

📖 Honestly, I feel as though I have spent my entire life learning both Japanese and English. Sometimes I find one language rising above the other, and code-switching is pretty common for me on a daily basis.

📖 But my language struggles pale when compared to the emotional battles I faced in seeking acceptance from my peers.

EXPERIENCING CULTURE SHOCK 2.0 (1995-1997)

Possessive Problems

I initially tried hiding my bilingual ability, especially when asked to speak English in certain situations. I could barely speak it when I got dunked into Japanese education. Though learning Japanese came easily for me as a child, it interfered with my English language development compared with peers who were native speakers of English only – especially when it came to syntactic and grammatical rules and forms. On my short visits to Indiana, my cousins noticed the difference in my behavior and how my English was suffering. I remember feeling somewhat isolated as I struggled to bond with them, despite our shared early years. I'd had a different upbringing since then. Even Grandpa said I had become 'unemotional' compared to my cousins.

I wasn't fully aware that I was behaving differently; it was kind of invisible to me. As more than half of my life had been in a culture alien to the people I was talking to, maybe my inability to express myself fully was inevitable. It was also frustrating. Looking back, I think it was a case of expectations. When opening a present at Christmas, for example, I was unable to give the exclamatory *oohs*, *aahs*, and *wows* that came from my cousins. I accepted the gift with quiet gratitude, doing my best to demonstrate a sincere thanks with a facial gesture. Similar to the British, the Japanese are known for being reserved and self-controlled. I absorbed this cultural nuance from my Japanese school immersion.

The absence of possessive pronouns in Japanese gave me the greatest problem in English. I would show ownership by stating a person's name in combination with the object being identified. It sounded weird when talking about myself or others in the third person – I would say things like 'Casey's ball' instead of 'my ball.' I would tell Mom things like 'I want Casey's candy' and when talking directly to her say 'Where is *Mom's* bag?' instead of 'Where is *your* bag?'

The Japanese particle *no* is a linguistic feature that indicates possession. Because there are no special forms other than *no* or の in Japanese to show ownership, I hadn't picked up on how to show possession in English and transferred Japanese grammar to my use of English language. I hadn't learned the words: my, his, her, your, their, and our. So I'd use a person's name in lieu of these possessive pronouns. In Japanese, you simply speak the possessive particle *no* after the owner's name or title and then follow it with the word for whatever object you mean. For example, 'Dad's book' would become '*papa no hon.*' If you wanted to say 'my book' you could say, '*Keeshi no hon*' or just take off the name and replace it with *boku* or *watashi* meaning 'I' or 'me' – so you could say '*boku no hon.*' Young children in Japan will default to using their name instead of *boku* or *watashi* when talking about their possessions. As the child grows up, they lose the habit of using their name when talking about themselves.[1]

Another aspect of English I struggled with was the past tense forms of irregular verbs. I had learned the rule for adding the inflected form 'ed' to indicate past tense, so I'd often say 'I goed to school' or 'I eated rice.' Also, there are no plural forms in Japanese. Whether you mention 'a book' or 'books,' the equivalent word is always *hon* – the word's plurality would be understood from the context. So you can imagine my monolingual grandpa's confusion at having his white American grandson tell him on an extended holiday trip, "I goed outside with Casey's ball and seed two squirrel!"

Island Hopping

If six years of living in Tokyo and experiencing that first culture shock at such a young age wasn't enough, I was destined to have another shock. I had finally found some kind of stability in my identity at age nine, but another change was looming.

Worried about my English language development and surprised at the high cost of an international bilingual education in Tokyo, my parents began exploring other employment opportunities outside of Japan. Looking back, I think Mom found an emotional connection with Japan and its people that Dad struggled to maintain. Although he appreciated the cultural aspects of living in Tokyo and visiting the countryside and knowing its people, Dad grew tired of the crowded trains and having to commute daily to various work assignments throughout Tokyo. It was also his viewpoint that in a prefecture with a population of 14 million people, you exist, but you don't really *live*. He preferred living in remote, rural places with scenes of nature and animals rather than concrete and people. Dad's mindset told him he was only visiting Japan for an extended period of time with every intention of returning to the United States. On the contrary, Mom, a true expat, could have spent the rest of her life in Japan. She was unafraid to face unknown challenges. Mom was a xenophile and had grown to love the Japanese culture and its people. Leaving a secure and rewarding teaching position added to her personal dilemma.

Two destinations were considered for our new home in the mid-1990s – Palau and Hawai'i. Imagine! Palauan[2] could have been my third language had my parents accepted employment offers to work in the Republic of Palau, part of Micronesia. Dad considered managing a local hotel while Mom was asked to start an English language school. We'd visited the island once. I remember playing with a fruit bat (a food delicacy), touring mangroves, visiting a scary crocodile farm, and watching a prisoner in a local jail skillfully carve a wooden storyboard – a popular folk craft. One day I was walking down a local street when I saw a man bleeding from his mouth. I ran to Dad.

"Look! Is something wrong with that man? He's chewing his mouth and blood is coming out," I whispered.

"It's okay, son. He's just having a snack. It's called betel nut," he said. This is when I learned about the Micronesian cultural appetite for betel nut, a palm seed chewed with leaves, lime, and other flavorings that acts as a stimulant and colors the mouth blood-red.

A final decision was made when my dad was hired as the training manager for the Ihilani Resort and Spa, then owned by Japan Airlines,[3] an impressive upscale resort property located on three man-made lagoons on the Westside of O'ahu. So, instead of relocating to Palau at the age of nine, where a new language challenge could have begun, I was brought back to the U.S.A. – to Hawai'i. My parents, and rightfully so, had based their decision on the fact that both my Japanese and English language skills might suffer if I were exposed to another new language.

While Mom and I were visiting family in Indiana, Dad prepared for our arrival by renting a modest plantation home in Mililani town, located in the center of the island. We entertained our Japanese friends Noriko and Shigeru at this home when they came to visit us with their two sons during our first Christmas there in 1995. It was here, too, that I celebrated my 10th birthday with a group of Mom's ESL students and new neighbors, including my future stepdad, Wade.

English – Illogical and Brutal

I was a frustrated and confused nine-year-old kid who wasn't used to English as the medium of instruction. I would grumble to my parents and generally felt helpless.

"Mom, I hate whoever made English spelling rules! English doesn't make any sense like Japanese does," I complained to her one day after being enrolled in school.

"I know, Casey. English is a very difficult language to learn, but you will by and by," she said, trying to comfort me. I wasn't convinced.

I didn't know how to spell words in English; I couldn't even read a Dr Seuss book on my own. I thought English was an illogical language and that the structure and rules of Japanese made more sense, especially with regard to spelling. My parents enrolled me in a Japanese school in Honolulu called *Rainbow Gakuen* on Saturdays, so as not to forget the language. I also went to the nearby Honbushin International Center[4] after school where Japanese cultural practices were celebrated. While this expansive hill-top facility provided a sort of comfort zone for a young boy raised in Japan, I was unable to bond with the local Hawaiian kids, even though they were mixed race or had Japanese ancestry. Naturally, most of them couldn't speak Japanese, but more importantly, their core cultural upbringing was 'local style' and unique to Hawai'i.[5] Years later, I had an encounter with one of these children at Hawaii Tokai International College.

"I knew a Casey long ago from the Honbushin," he said to me after our introductions.

Although I didn't remember him, it was clear that I was the person he remembered – and from the tone of his voice and his body language, not in a positive way. It was like reliving those awkward early years where I struggled to fit in. I felt uneasy and regretted not having developed a better relationship with this person back then.

Mom had to tutor me almost daily in phonics, reading, and writing and came to my first school, Hoʻala, in person to do so. How embarrassing. I was the only student whose mother had to be present, take me out of the main classroom to an adjoining room, and spend a few hours teaching me how to sound out the English alphabet and learn to read words. I attended three different Hawaiʻi schools in the space of two years from age nine to eleven in an effort to master English – not to mention fit in. First, I attended the Hoʻala School on weekdays. Although I slowly began to make improvements in my English language acquisition, my cultural understanding had a long way to go. During my transition from Japanese culture to local American culture in the islands, I recall having difficulties with my schoolmates. One boy, who I'd become close with, one day said he didn't want to be my friend anymore. Confused and feeling abandoned, I pushed him for an explanation, which led to a 3-way meeting with our homeroom teacher. Evidently, he had been ridiculed by other students for hanging out with me.

I remember one especially painful bullying experience in Hawaiʻi when a group of boys challenged me on the playground during recess.

"Hey! New boy! Why you so funny, huh?" the leader of the group called out.

"Hi, I just arrived from Japan," I replied.

"Something wrong with your head?" a boy asked. "You stupid, yeah?"

Suddenly, one boy reached out, grabbed the middle fingers of both of my hands, and started bending them backwards.

I tried to headbutt him, which gave me an opening to run back to the school building. I was suspended. Because there was only one of me, and four of them, their version of the story was believed over mine. As a result, I attempted fourth grade at a second private elementary school called Hanalani. Science and Social Studies were particularly difficult subjects for me there. I also had to learn to recite Bible verses. Because I couldn't understand, I didn't pay attention. This resulted in bad grades and once again I was mocked by the other students for being different.

Finally, I repeated fourth grade at a nearby public primary school, Kipapa Elementary. I felt the most comfortable in this public elementary school and found I could blend in with the multicultural student population. Maybe I also fitted in because I was surrounded by other students all with their own problems, or because the expectations might have been lower. I had a kind teacher, Mrs Kaer, who gave me room to explore my own identity. It was there that I began to feel equal to my peers and even wrote a short story titled *The Three Little Menehune*,[6] which was published into book form along with stories from other students. Mrs Kaer wrote these words on an old report card I found from that time: "Casey did, on his own, ask to take a spelling test and on the second test got one word correct. For this I acknowledge Casey for stepping forward to accept this challenge. Casey's challenge lies in overcoming the language barrier and not to use it as an excuse to not participate in class." Spelling was a huge problem for me. For example, the Japanese word for bicycle is *jidensha*. When I tried to spell it in English I would write 'byesikuru.' It just made sense that way.

Honestly, I feel as though I have spent my entire life learning both Japanese and English. Sometimes I find one language rising above the other, and code-switching is pretty common for me on a daily basis. I still make grammatical errors in both languages. Trying to balance my proficiency level in each has always been one of my greatest personal challenges. But my language struggles pale when compared to the emotional battles I faced in seeking acceptance from my peers.

A Big Decision

When Mom and Dad married in 1985, my grandparents were elated and thought it was a perfect match since both were from white middle-class families with a Catholic religious background. Unfortunately, their move to Japan for Mom's employment wasn't good for their marriage. As they each expanded their individual global perspective, the commonalities they'd shared in Indiana soon evaporated. As a consequence, my parents gradually drifted apart, focusing their attention instead on their respective careers, with vacation trips abroad as a distraction. Although they tried to work on their marriage in Hawai'i, little did Dad know that his decision to choose that particular rental property in Mililani would affect Mom's destiny, as she would eventually fall in love with the landlord's son, Wade.

The resort where Dad worked became my personal playground where I enjoyed the lagoons, tennis courts, hotel facilities, and amenities. I spent many hot sunny days at the beach learning how to body surf and how to play golf with Dad. I was spoiled. When the Japan bubble burst in the early

90s,[7] the Japanese extension college, Kansai Gakuen, where Mom had been teaching in Honolulu, closed its Hawai'i campus. Soon after, she was offered another position, this time working for Southern Illinois University's extension campus in Niigata, Japan. Even though I welcomed the idea of returning to Japan, I knew it would be a difficult move for me. Absorbing the impacts of my parents' divorce and facing radical life adjustments was emotional. Not only would I be leaving a new friend, Kai, who I'd become close with in Hawai'i, but I'd also be leaving my biological dad behind to live in Japan with Mom and Wade.

I remember the last night I spent with Dad at his new Mililani condo before our departure back to Japan. We performed our usual routine, where we enjoyed a hot home-cooked meal while playing chess on his black-and-green marble chess set and listening to our favorite song, *Angel Eyes*, by Jim Brickman. As the time for departure grew near, Mom came in to get me as Wade waited outside in the car. Rain was pouring down, and tears welled up in my eyes. I became emotional and I began to cry at the thought of saying goodbye to Dad. I would miss his playful wrestling, tight hugs, and warm smile. I would miss our routines, such as sharing a French toast breakfast on the *lanai* [patio] while soaking up the warm rays of sunshine through the trees. I was sad. The three of us cried together as we shared our last moment together as a family. Japan had been the trigger for Mom and Dad splitting up. Living there had exposed the profound realization of how different they really were and how different each had embraced the experience. I was not only caught between cultures; now I was also caught between parents.

Synthesis of Identity

Wade was Hawaiian at heart. Early on, everything we learned about Hawai'i came from him. Mom called him her "Hawaiian Samurai." He taught us about the foods, the music, the history, the significant places, and the cultural values of the Hawaiian people.[8] His generation was the last to go 'crabbing' using hand-held nets in O'ahu's inland streams. A free diver in his youth, he remembered the abundance of sea life and the clean ocean waters of his childhood before ecological disruption. But it was their shared knowledge of and interest in Japanese food, culture, and customs that cemented Mom and Wade's early friendship. Wade had lost his linguistic heritage; Mom could communicate in Japanese at a higher skill level than he could. She learned quickly how underlying cultural ideas, beliefs, and values played a significant role in their relationship. Maybe as a result of his *samurai* lineage, Wade had an alpha male personality, with a superior, male-dominating role within the family.

I was going to miss Hawai'i a lot. Before Mom, Wade, and I left for Japan, we rented a house on top of a mountain in Pupukea on the North Shore of O'ahu, which was an ideal place for me to run free and explore. The house was located in the middle of a tropical rainforest, and although we were only there for a little more than a year, I would often go hiking and pick avocados, strawberry guava, passion fruit, and mountain apples. The backyard of our home was exciting and felt like my own personal Amazon jungle. Wade used his carpentry skills to build a hutch where I had some pet rabbits. Occasionally, wild pigs would run through our yard, which was the size of a football pitch. This is the home where I remember celebrating my second Christmas in Hawai'i when my Grandma Jane and Uncle Dave and family visited us during the cold Indiana winter holidays. What a great time we all had. I remember taking the family to the Honbushin Center to pound *mochi* [9] for the New Year's holiday, and the sweet and earthy smell of the rice being steamed while lifting the heavy wooden mallet to pound the mixture into *mochi*. During that visit, we also planted bright red and pink impatiens[10] together along the west side of our house. We went sightseeing to Pearl Harbor, Waimea Valley, and the Polynesian Cultural Center. Being around all this beauty and appreciating it after years in a metropolis, I remember making a promise to myself that I would return.

As I became accustomed to my new stepfather, arguments broke out about what Wade perceived as my lack of discipline – over such things as my study habits and attention to household chores. Wade was the product of a fiercely strict father of Okinawan descent who was emotionally distant and intensely self-disciplined. Whenever he'd asked his father a 'how' or 'why' question about anything, the response had always been "Go read." Never would his dad do it for him. In a similar way, but to a much lesser extent, I suffered the same fate. Wade represented, rather synthesized, my Japanese cultural background, and I could identify with him on many levels. He lectured me and encouraged me to reflect on my decisions, to seek knowledge, and find answers on my own. At the same time, his quiet steadiness coupled with meticulous attention to any task taught me to face my own challenges head-on. As I mentioned earlier, Wade could fix anything.

He could do anything. He certainly tried to adapt to his new role as a stepdad, and, to his credit, he was determined to make a man of his stepson, albeit with a son who could be a pain in the *okole*, which is Hawaiian for backside or butt.

Mom, on the other hand, having been raised in an era of women's liberation, was up for challenging his traditional thinking with lectures of equality – though, more wisely, she'd often tolerate his illusions. Her ability to 'anticipatory manage' prevented some large-scale domestic conflicts. This term, originally coined by University of Hawai'i Professor Emeritus Takie Lebra and described by Bruce E. Barnes in his book *Culture, Conflict, and Mediation in the Asian Pacific*, is defined as the ability 'to preventatively manage conflict before the conflict is even generated.'[11] On numerous occasions, I watched how Mom would also use a 'negative communication' approach in dealing with arguments that she and my stepdad would have, and vice versa.[12] Cultural views of 'silence' may have been instrumental in working through these conflicts as well. From Mom's perspective and cultural background, silence is not 'golden' and is an uncomfortable presence in a relationship. In contrast, for my stepdad, silence is familiar and normal and not to be considered as negative energy.

Probably one of the biggest areas of conflict between my mom and stepdad was with respect to the virtue of humility. Raised nearly half a world apart, my stepdad would sometimes, in an angry moment, accuse my mother of being 'me, myself and I' or of having a high *maka maka* attitude, which in Hawaiian literally means 'face higher than the other.' It reminded me of the paradoxical American proverb:

'The squeaky wheel gets the grease.' Raised in Indiana, Mom grew up with the concept of individual rights and competitive success. She delighted in giving her opinion and standing up for what she believed in. My stepdad, on the other hand, lived by the aforementioned Japanese proverb – 'The nail that sticks up gets pounded into place' – which is a totally contradictory statement and which expresses the exact opposite of the 'squeaky wheel' American proverb.[13] Growing up in Japan, I remember speaking up in class when the teacher asked a question. Later I learned that the other kids were annoyed I'd shown off; it was only okay to answer when called upon. Wade tended to be more reserved when it came to sharing his thoughts and ideas. At the age of 11, I was bracing myself to go home – to Japan – with this new Asian male adult figure in my life.

NOTES

1 I suspect this phenomenon is due to children hearing only their first names spoken by the adults and peers in their life. Furthermore, adults seldom use personal pronouns and typically refer to themselves and their positions by using their title or relationship to the child.

2 Palauan is a Malayo-Polynesian language from the Austronesian language family.

3 The JW Marriott Ihilani Resort and Spa closed in 2015, underwent extensive renovations, and became the Four Seasons Resort Oʻahu at Ko Olina. It is the first Four Seasons property on the island.

4   The Honbushin International Center is a religious center
     that teaches peace through the blessings of God and offers
     a variety of unique services and events.

5   Although Hawai'i became the 50th state in 1959, its 'mixed
     plate' cultural heritage is different from the mainland.
     Nearly a quarter of its population identifies as multiracial,
     with ties to two or more races. Pidgin English, a Hawaiian
     creole language, is an official language of the islands and
     developed as a result of mingling ethnicities during the
     sugarcane plantation era. Following the arrival of Chinese
     contract workers in 1852, other groups including Japanese,
     Okinawan, Portuguese, Puerto Rican, Korean, African
     (from Cape Verde), and Filipino came to Hawai'i to work
     on the plantations.

6   *Menehune* are legendary pre-Polynesian residents of
     Hawai'i that resemble dwarfs or gnomes. Residents of the
     deep tropical rain forests of the islands, they are said to be
     great craftsmen and only appear in the wee hours of the
     night.

7   The Japanese economic era from 1986 to 1991 in which
     real estate prices and stock market values were greatly
     inflated, resulting in accelerated asset prices and
     overconfident economic activity. When the 'economic
     bubble' burst in 1992, the Japanese economy suffered a
     major decline over the next decade.

8   Although Wade is ethnically Japanese-Okinawan, he is
     also culturally Hawaiian, having been educated in
     Hawai'i's multicultural educational system with its
     inherent traditions and customs. He identifies with

Hawaiʻi more than with Japan. He had been unable to communicate with his grandmother who spoke no English while he spoke no Japanese.

9   *Mochi* is Japanese pounded rice; (sticky) rice cake; usually eaten at New Year and on other special occasions. It has a super-chewy, soft and dough-like texture and can be filled with sweet red bean paste or other fillings.

10   Impatiens are shade-loving flowers that come in a variety of colors. They are known as busy Lizzy by the British.

11   Barnes explains by giving this example: "Victim A may express frustration or anger to B, but does so in a negative way, i.e. by not communicating it. Instead of confronting B, A avoids seeing or contacting B, thereby transmitting to B how upset A is and how strongly A disagrees with B." Barnes, B. E. (2006). *Culture, Conflict, and Mediation in the Asian Pacific.* (p. 49). University Press of America.

12   Ibid., p. 49.

13   They have always been able to reconcile their conflicts. They celebrated their 25th anniversary together in 2021.

QR code for
Chapter Three
Photographs

CULTURAL SYNOPSIS

CHAPTER FOUR
Adjusting to a Second Culture

This chapter reflects the third stage of culture shock, called adjustment. Although there were some bumps, I can confidently say that I was well on my way to adopting Japanese culture as part of my identity.

- I was considered a *kikokushijo* [returnee child] and was expected to assimilate back into the Japanese educational system without a hiccup.

- My cultural identity at this time was influenced almost entirely by the Asian environment I was being raised in. All of my friends were Japanese. But my identity felt like it was constantly teeter-tottering between East and West as on many occasions I traveled, sometimes alone, back and forth between Japan and America.

- It was at this time that I became obsessed with drawing intricate mazes, which probably reflected the path of my life up to that point.

- Kanazawa was a time I really felt at home. When asked my nationality back then, I often said I was Japanese, not American.

- I felt comfortable at *Takaodai* Junior High School in Kanazawa wearing the required *gakuran*, a uniform modeled on the uniforms of the European navy.

- I had formed a lasting bond, not only with my friends but with Japan and a culture that had become second nature.

- When people cross borders and get to know one another, it closes the door to hatred forever.

- I had finally adjusted to my second culture and I didn't want to leave.

ADJUSTING TO A SECOND CULTURE (1997–2000)

Waffle Breakfasts with Yuko

I was raised from ages three to nine in Tokyo, a city with neon-lit streets, crowded sidewalks, and towering skyscrapers. Walking through this metropolis, especially when underground, made me feel insignificant within the endless waves of people going about their daily business. Despite the mass of people, I couldn't help but wonder in awe at the mutual regard the Japanese had for others. When I was around eight years old, I remember Mom accidentally leaving her purse at a bus stop in the district of Sangenjaya and then returning hours later to look for it. To her relief, and surprise, the purse was still there with everything inside it. Of course, that was the early 90s and things may be different now. But this Japanese collective behavior had a strong impact on my moral upbringing as it taught me about honesty and doing one's best not to inconvenience others.

In the depths of this concrete jungle, you could still find the ancient and traditional Japan: age-old brown wooden temples and red-gated shrines, small Mom and Pop-type stalls selling *tatami* [grass floor mats], *tabi* [footwear] *tofu* [bean curd], *kimonos* [traditional T-shaped garments], *futon* [floor bedding], and other crafts along with a multitude of *ramen* [noodle] shops and eateries. My normal 'everyday' experience of Japan had been playing video games inside my Tokyo apartment, riding my bicycle in local parks, taking trains, and walking only five minutes to my elementary school.

When I left Hawai'i and returned to Japan in 1997 at the age of 11 for my mother's new teaching destination, we moved to a small farming village surrounded by rice fields. I enrolled in a country elementary school for 5th grade. I was considered a *kikokushijo* [returnee child] and was expected to assimilate back into the Japanese educational system without a hiccup.[1] It was challenging, to say the least.

Located in Niigata prefecture northwest of Tokyo, on Japan's largest and most populated island of Honshu, Nakajo was a small rural farming town famous for cultivating *koshihikari* rice. It's now known as Tainai City. My walk to and from school was long: one hour there and one hour back. I trudged through several feet of snow past white blanketed rice fields in winter, and grassy green paddies during early summer.

In Nakajo, Mom met her best friend, Yuko. Yuko worked at the Southern Illinois University Carbondale (SIUC) library in Niigata and held legendary weekend waffle breakfasts.

Looking back, Yuko provided the emotional support the three of us needed to thrive in such a harsh climate as Niigata. Growing up as a city boy in Tokyo, I had never seen *kamemushi* [stink bugs], *mamushi* [venomous pit vipers], and *tanuki* [racoon dogs]. She showed us the ropes when it came to surviving in this rural mountainous area of Japan, known as *yukiguni* [2] [snow country]. My hair had grown long. I could almost tie it up in a samurai topknot. Ragged in appearance, I must have resembled one of the local *tanuki* when she met me – thankfully, she didn't treat me like one.

Yuko would often let us borrow her car to pick up *tōyu* [kerosene] for our heater or she would bring homemade muffins and bread to our campus housing unit. It was cold in Nakajo. Wade saw his first real snowfall here as snowflakes blanketed the already white Japanese village. He was as happy as when drinking *nihonshu*,[3] the local rice wine more commonly known as *sake*. With our arms reaching toward the night sky, Yuko, Wade, and I went out snowflake catching. Slipping and sliding down the secluded lane in front of our university housing units, it felt like we were in a Disney film. Wade soon broke the spell by asking Yuko: "Do you have a snow shovel for Casey?"

Yuko was instrumental in helping Wade locate his long-lost Japanese lineage on his mother's side.[4] We met his blood relatives and visited the family gravesite to pay our respects. To Wade's delight, the gravesite was located across the highway from a Kikusui Sake brewing factory in the city of Shibata, about 15 kilometers from Nakajo. In the short time we lived there, Yuko did more than her fair share of translating documents and interpreting conversations. Yuko was an insider whose love of world cultures and people infected all those she encountered. Through her support and friendship, she helped me to make the most of a tumultuous period in my young life.

My Personal Mr Miyagi

As a family, we were an enigma in Japan. Wade looked like a Japanese national yet could not speak the language. I looked like a foreigner, but I could speak Japanese like a native. Often, in a restaurant, a waiter or waitress would approach Wade only to end up speaking with me. A Japanese man who owned a local restaurant once raised his voice at Wade when Wade stayed quiet as I spoke for him. I guess the man felt shunned by Wade's silence. Or maybe he'd just never come across a Japanese-looking man being spoken for by a fluent young *gaijin* [foreigner] child.

Wade was not an affectionate man, particularly in a public place. But he showed his love to Mom and me through his actions. He loved to barbecue, even during Niigata's harsh, snowy winters, heating up an ice-cold grill to sizzle pork sausages or steak. We'd routinely stop at a country convenience store for afterschool drinks and snacks as he accompanied me on my long and grueling one-hour walk home from school across Niigata's rice fields. My treat of choice was a vanilla ice cream ball wrapped in soft *mochi* called *Yukimi Daifuku*. It was a heavenly combination of creamy filling and chewy outside. To wash it down, my favorite go-to beverages were non-fizzy soft drinks – peach water and Calpis. Of course, Wade would always get his One

Cup Ozeki *sake* to sip on while I enjoyed my sugar high. Surrounded by an endless sea of rice fields, Wade and I would sit on a faded turquoise bench outside the convenience store and stare at the scenery in silence as we enjoyed our favorite treats.

It was great to be back in Japan and have a thoughtful neighbor like Yuko, but it was still difficult fitting in with the local kids. They were country boys; I was a *gaijin* city kid – and I had just come from America. Having small scuffles during recess and cleaning time was common. I grew accustomed to not only verbal, but physical abuse as well. After school, boys would throw snowballs spiked with rocks and shout, "Go back to America!" Wade understood the challenge I was going through and advised me on handling difficult situations, like when a group of boys tried to ambush me on a quiet backroad. He volunteered to meet me after school and accompany me home on foot or bicycle whenever he thought I might be in trouble. In many ways, as I became Wade's personal translator, he became like my personal Mr Miyagi from the 1984 film *The Karate Kid* – Wade even caught a fly with his chopsticks once.

In the film, old Miyagi-sensei taught young Daniel a philosophy of life. It's a story of discovery, where Daniel eventually learns to follow his heart and mind, not just his hands. The similarities with Wade go deeper, though: Gichin Funakoshi, the father of modern Japanese karate, is an Okinawan ancestor of my stepdad. He was not only a master of karate but also a scholar of Chinese classical writing. Calligraphy was a required subject during my early academic years, so I had a better understanding of why Master

Funakoshi believed an intimate connection linked Oriental concepts, languages, and thought patterns with physical skills.

For example, 書道, which is the Chinese character for the Japanese word *shodō* [calligraphy], can be literally translated as *sho* meaning 'write' and *dō* meaning 'path or way.' Similarly, *karate-dō* can be translated as *kara* meaning 'open or empty' and *te* meaning 'hand(s).' A meaningful translation would be 'the way of open hands.' Like calligraphy, the practice of martial arts is not so focused on 'art' as many in the West might think, but rather on one's 'path or way.'

Just as the practice of calligraphy directed the 'way' in my thinking process, Wade opened my eyes to see a 'path.' Among the many dinner-time lectures from Wade that I sat through, the one about dealing with bullies was timely and cemented itself in my memory. Wade taught me to confront bullies by helping me to believe in myself and to rely on my inner energy or *ki* (気). Even though there were times when I did get aggressive with these antagonists, I preferred to deal with them verbally or to simply avoid conflict.

Teeter-Tottering Between East and West

My cultural identity at this time was influenced almost entirely by the Asian environment I was being raised in. All of my friends were Japanese. But my identity felt like it was constantly teeter-tottering between East and West as on many occasions I traveled, sometimes alone, back and forth between Japan and America. During extended school vacations, Wade would drive me to either Kansai or Narita airports so I could visit Dad in America. While other Japanese kids in the neighborhood weren't even allowed to use the train alone to travel to Tokyo, I'd be placed in the care of a flight attendant who would watch over me until I was met at the arrival gate by my biological father on the other side of the Pacific Ocean.

Over the years, I visited Dad in California, New Mexico and, later, Oregon. I remember one long seven-hour flight across to Reno, Nevada, where Dad met me with a smiling face and a big American hug. On that trip to Sugar Bowl Resort, his place of employment at the time, we rented a couple of kayaks for two days and went down a two-mile-long lake on a cold and windy day (Dad's idea of fun). At first it was calm, but as we paddled further, the water became choppy and violent. I took a break on some rocks to avoid capsizing and to munch on a power bar and remembered what my dad had been like when we lived in Japan. Dad wasn't afraid of danger. He once jumped off the train platform onto a subway track in Tokyo to save a drunk man who'd accidentally fallen from the platform. Of course, no trains were coming at the time, but still, for him to jump off the platform made an impression on a young son raised in a culture where dramatic acts of bravado were discouraged. Unlike Dad, who was being adventurous, I was cautious. Back in the water paddling against the wind, I thought to myself, *If I were ever in that situation, would I have the guts to jump?*

I spent an entire month with Dad on that visit. We played basketball, rented movies, and hiked mountains. During my winter visits, we went skiing together. Looking back, I feel that most of my vacation time was spent with Dad, while my education was spent with Mom and Wade. However, all three of my parents are equally important to me, and they each taught me many valuable life lessons as I navigated the path of my bicultural identity crisis.

Despite their different influences on me, all three of my parents valued travel. They had high educational expectations for me, and traveling was a part of that overall educational experience. I remember on a trip to the island of Pangkor, Malaysia, that I was amazed by the flying sparks coming from an older man pounding a piece of metal in the middle of the street. Most parents would probably yank their kids away from such a situation, but mine valued these moments of cultural encounter and encouraged their curious child to pick up a hammer to batter a piece of a rusty old car part. Curiosity also has its downsides, though: on the same trip, I had to visit a local doctor twice in one week after being stung by a jellyfish and falling into an open drainage ditch.

Of course, I traveled within Japan, too, including visits to the historical and cultural cities of Kyoto and Nara, where I saw the iconic statue of the *Daibutsu* or Great Buddha. While in Nara, I was frightened by an overly aggressive domesticated deer who roamed the park property searching for handouts (deer biscuits) from tourists. Although these memories may seem insignificant to some, as a child, these experiences were tattooed into my inner consciousness and added weight to each side of my cultural scale.

One of my most memorable and epic adventures was climbing to the summit of the sacred mountain Mount Fuji with my parents and Uncle Tony, who was visiting us in Japan at the time. As we trekked up the mountain slope, we passed many elderly Japanese people who were in the later years of life. Climbing Mount Fuji was not just a tourist activity or significant cultural experience – it's considered to be a spiritual pilgrimage for many Japanese people. With the sun beating down on us, our legs getting tired, and the air thinning, we considered turning back as we stood on the side of the trail.

"*Ganbatte!*" [You can do it!] shouted an old Japanese man passing us.

We smiled and thanked him in Japanese for his encouragement: "*Arigatou gozaimasu*" [a formal thank you].

It was at this moment I was reminded of the Japanese concept of *gaman*.[5][6] An important virtue to Japanese society, *gaman* refers to the ability to endure. The concept, which is taught in Zen Buddhism, teaches how one must persevere through trials or hardship with patience and dignity.

Leaving the thought of retreat behind us, we continued on our trek toward the summit. Mom and I spent a night sleeping next to others packed like sardines in a large cabin that was three-quarters of the way up the mountain and just visible among the dense clouds. Dad and Uncle Tony slept outside in the cold, parallel to the clouds, while keeping an eye on a purple-hued lightning storm far off in the distance. Just before sunrise we were back on the trail, ready to greet Japan's iconic and glorious red rising sun.

Generally, the Japanese people were very courteous and welcoming to me and my family. There was a genuine curiosity about who we were and where we came from. Many enjoyed trying to speak the little English that they knew and tried hard to communicate with us. I remember two separate occasions, however, when we experienced outright discrimination. The first was at a small restaurant somewhere in rural

Japan, where we were asked to leave the restaurant based on our American nationality.[78] The second experience happened in Yokohama while sightseeing one weekend. An older Japanese man in a gruff and rude tone gestured to my parents to get me and leave the premises. Because this was such an uncommon occurrence, my parents quickly responded to his request and we all left. We never really understood why he asked us to leave, particularly as I wasn't misbehaving. Perhaps he held old animosities toward Caucasian-looking foreigners. However, these negative experiences never dampened our love of traveling within Japan or our view of the Japanese people. My family and I had already learned that in Japanese culture it was best to leave rather than make a scene. We also understood that rudeness was a problem with some individuals, not all Japanese people. We knew about nails getting pounded into place and that our Japanese friends would be as horrified as we were. Stereotyping a culture based on selective experiences is unfair.

Light at the End of the Maze

I moved again in 1998 for sixth grade when Mom accepted a teaching position at Kanazawa Institute of Technology, an engineering university. With a 15th-century castle over-looking the city and well-preserved Edo-era architecture, Kanazawa is located on the west coast of Japan's central island of Honshu along the Sea of Japan. I was much better at making friends here. However, I do remember it wasn't perfect. As is typical at Japanese schools, students were required to exchange their outdoor shoes for indoor shoes upon entering the building. Each student had their individual shoebox where they would store their footwear. Twice at the end of the school day, I was met with piercing pain when I placed my foot into a shoe filled with thumbtacks. I asked my male friends and they suspected it might have been some of the girls who didn't think so well of me and wanted me to quit going to the school. Lucky for me, I bonded with my sixth-grade teacher and became obsessed with playing sports, especially soccer. I developed close friendships with several of my male classmates with whom I later entered junior high school. It was in junior high school that I remember being ecstatic to win a relay event at the school's annual *undokai* [sports day][9] for my red team. Those same good friends later traveled to Indiana to visit me.

I felt comfortable at *Takaodai* Junior High School in Kanazawa wearing the required *gakuran*, a uniform modeled on the uniforms of the European navy. It consisted of long black pants and a jacket with a standing collar. The jacket fastened from top-to-bottom with golden buttons embossed with the school emblem. Wearing this uniform was a sign of earned maturity and educational promotion all over Japan.[10] It was at this time that I became obsessed with drawing intricate mazes, which probably reflected the path of my life up to that point. I spent hours alone in my room creating passageways that connected, blocked, surprised, and led to various adventures.

Kanazawa was expensive for us, though, particularly as we lived only on a teacher's salary. I remember Wade once went to a pawnshop to hawk his G-shock watch and make some extra money for me to buy that middle school uniform.

Another day, while upstairs in my bedroom with Mom rummaging through some pockets in a coat closet, we found a 500-yen coin (equivalent to about $5) which was like buried treasure at the time. With this, Mom and I went to a nearby store and splurged on Japanese snacks and treats. I bought loads of 10-yen corn puff rods called *umaibō* meaning 'good tasty stick' that came in flavors like corn soup, cheese, teriyaki burger, salami, vegetable salad, chicken curry, beef tongue, pizza, and more. To satisfy my sweet tooth, I loaded up on packages of Pocky – thin biscuit sticks coated in chocolate.

We rented an older two-storey traditional Japanese house while in Kanazawa. The entire living space downstairs and upstairs was *tatami* mat [rush grass flooring], with the exception of the kitchen and *genkan* [entrance], where Japanese people keep shoes and talk to neighbors who drop by. The house didn't have a Western-style toilet but an elongated squat-style porcelain hole in the ground. It required strong knees and good balance. During the winters the restroom was not heated and was the coldest room in the house. It was my job during the winter to wake up first and go outside to manually pump kerosene into a small tank and heat up the living room and kitchen. In contrast, the *ofuro* [bathroom] transformed into one of the warmest places in the house when filled with scalding hot water for our family baths – meaning that the entire household would use the same water, each in turn, after first showering with warm water at a hand-held waist-high faucet while sitting on a stool.

During my seventh-grade year at Takanawadai Junior High School, I was elected class president. There were two factors that led up to this moment. First was when a couple of students and I were called to the front of the class to write *kanji* [Chinese characters] with the correct stroke order. I was the only one to write them in the correct order even though I was not Japanese. That impressed the teacher and my 40-odd classmates. Second, it was probably my newfound popularity and blond hair. I regretted being appointed class president because I didn't adequately fulfill my role. I was more concerned with enjoying school life than attending meetings and advocating for my classmates in student government. As a result, my popularity soon declined. But I still had a special group of friends to hang out with during this time. We visited each other's homes, sang karaoke, and even hid from the police inside a carwash one late night to avoid getting into trouble. As young teenagers, we rebelled by doing things naughty young boys typically do, like smoking a cigarette or buying an adult magazine. I knew we were breaking cultural rules of conduct, but risks are only scary when you don't have friends taking them along with you.

Kanazawa was a time I really felt at home. When asked my nationality back then, I often said I was Japanese, not American. The evening before our flight back home to Indiana from Kanazawa in 2000, I asked Mom to drive me to my junior high school for one last time. The building was dark and empty. It was late at night. I sat silently in the car, staring at the campus, with only the schoolyard spotlights illuminating the dark buildings. Sadness fell upon me like a coastal fog. These walls housed some of my fondest memories yet; I needed this last goodbye.

The long flight to Indiana the next day felt like heading for outer space. I was flying to a complete unknown. I'd formed a lasting bond, not only with my friends but with Japan and a culture that had become second nature. When people cross borders and get to know one another, it closes the door to hatred forever. I had finally adjusted to my second culture and I didn't want to leave.

———————————

NOTES

1   *Kikokushijo* is a Japanese language term referring to children who have lived and been educated abroad and then return to Japan. In my case, I was also returning to Japan after living in Hawai'i for two years. Generally, the TCK experience is not recognized in the Japanese educational system, and students are expected to 'fall in line' immediately upon returning.

2   *Yukiguni* or (雪国) literally translates to 'snow country' in English: (雪) *yuki* meaning snow, and (国) *kuni* meaning country. Phonologically the 'K' in kuni changes to 'G' due to following the word *yuki*.

3   *Nihonshu* (日本酒) translates into 'Japanese alcohol' but is more commonly known as *sake* (酒). Technically, *sake* just means alcohol and is commonly misunderstood as the word for Japanese alcohol. Traditionally, *nihonshu* is made from polishing and fermenting rice.

4   Wade's maternal Japanese grandfather had immigrated to Hawai'i from Niigata prefecture in the late 1800s. As the story goes, he was prompted to leave Japan when the Kaji River flooded the region, destroying the rice fields. As a

farmer, he sought work in the sugarcane plantations of Hawai'i in order to make a living. His brother chose to remain in Japan, so the family had essentially been separated by distance and personal choice after the natural disaster.

5   What is sometimes misunderstood by the West as an introverted personality within the Japanese psyche may actually be the practice of *gaman* in an individual. For example, in Japan, there is a term that means 'death by overwork' called *karōshi*. Westerners may view an individual who works so hard as to risk their health as showing submissive or introverted behavior, whereas the Japanese worker may view his or her action as *gaman*.

6   Littler, J. (2019, March 19). *The art of perseverance: How gaman defined Japan.* BBC. https://www.bbc.com/worklife/article/20190319-the-art-of-perseverance-how-gaman-defined-japan

7   As mentioned in footnote 12 from *Chapter Two*, I have found from my experience that Japanese nationals are less likely to show racist attitudes on the surface than Japanese-Americans. On the contrary, Japanese nationals hold deep-seated discriminatory practices toward foreigners due to their cultural homogeneity. Common examples of this include the difficulty foreigners face in securing rental housing, obtaining higher-level positions, and being accepted by Japanese extended family in international marriage relationships. Although laws exist that address equal opportunity, discrimination toward foreigners continues to be apparent. Allow me to qualify these

comments by saying that there are variables to consider with Japanese nationals, such as age, location, and experience.

8   Funakoshi, M. (2017, March 30). *Foreigners in Japan face significant levels of discrimination, survey shows.* Reuters. https://www.reuters.com/article/us-japan-discrimination-foreign/foreigners-in-japan-face-significant-levels-of-discrimination-survey-shows-idUSKBN1720GP

9   *Undokai* in Japan, unlike sports days in the U.S., is usually composed of two teams, a red team and a white team, who compete against each other throughout the event. Individual competition is not emphasized as strongly as the group effort.

10   All across Japan, the majority of middle schools and high schools require uniforms. Private elementary schools usually require uniforms. Some public elementary schools also require them, but the majority of public elementary students can wear casual clothes.

QR code for
Chapter Four
photographs

CULTURAL SYNOPSIS

CHAPTER FIVE
Experiencing Reverse Culture Shock

This chapter reflects the fifth stage of culture shock, referred to as reverse culture shock or re-entry shock. Having just left Japan for the second time, my cultural identity was once more rattled when I returned to the American Midwest, where I was born.

- Relocating to Indiana was traumatic. I was a foreigner in my own country – even my own state.

- When I arrived in Indiana in early 2000, I was enrolled into an Intensive English Program (IEP), where my mother was also employed as an instructor. I found myself in a familiar setting at the American Language Academy – the only American in a class of foreigners. But this time it was a multicultural group rather than a homogeneous one.

- Empathetic to my culture shock, Mom registered me for eighth grade at the Indiana Japanese Language School on Saturdays. Here I was again, the only American white boy in a Japanese school.

- At the age of 14, I enrolled into the International School of Indiana (ISI). One of the biggest shocks I experienced was all the hugging and kissing. Coming from Japan, where intimate affection is rarely displayed, I was overwhelmed by the sense of touch.

- I was frustrated, struggling with the language and watching a barrier develop between me and my classmates.

EXPERIENCING REVERSE CULTURE SHOCK (2000-2005)

Logograms, Phonics, and Math, Oh My!

Relocating to Indiana was traumatic. By the age of 14, I'd already attended nine different schools, counting all of those in Japan and Hawai'i. My biological father, grandparents, uncles, aunts, and cousins warmly welcomed me home to the Hoosier state, but I felt awkward. I was uncomfortable adjusting to the American educational system and trying to make new friends yet again. A front-page feature article published in *The Indianapolis Star* on December 11, 2000, aptly explained my struggle to fit in.[1] This article also contained an insightful quote from Ruth Van Reken: "Being born in one country and raised in another has benefits, but assimilation can be problematic. Half the battle is understanding that you're not a freak. It's just that your experience is different."[2]

The Midwest U.S. environment was strange compared to my upbringing in Japan. Rules for making friends were different, as were the interests of U.S. teenagers. I realized I still had limited proficiency when it came to reading, writing, and understanding idioms in the English language. I kept wondering where the cake was each time someone said "it's a piece of cake!" Mathematics, on the other hand, was a little easier for me than other subjects, except for word problems. I think this is due, in part, to the practice of memorizing pictures (logograms) rather than memorizing sounds (phonics).[3]

I remember teachers in Japan during elementary school focusing on *how* I solved a problem, requiring me to perform the long calculations by hand, in contrast to teachers in Indiana who focused on whether I got the right answer or not. In Japan, writing out the *shiki* [formula] was more important than arriving at a solution, whereas in the U.S., the final solution was more important than the problem-solving phase. This knowledge of math gave me enough confidence to take some higher-level math courses, sparked my interest in physics, and helped me achieve academically. Unable to find a level playing field socially and linguistically, I could at least compete with my peers in mathematics. As for the other subjects, I felt inferior. I was frustrated, struggling with the language and watching a barrier develop between me and my classmates.

Multicultural Discoveries

When I arrived in Indiana in early 2000, I was enrolled into an Intensive English Program (IEP), where my mother was also employed as an instructor. The American Language Academy (ALA) was located on the Butler University campus in Indianapolis. Because my English language skills were inferior to my American peers, she thought I would benefit from classes in reading comprehension, writing, vocabulary development, and English grammar before enrolling me into an American high school. I entered level four of a six-level multi-skills program. I was able to track my scores on the Test of English as a Foreign Language (TOEFL) and the Test of English for International Communication (TOEIC). I went backwards on the TOEFL with a total test score of 540 in December of 2000 to a 507 in March of 2001. My TOEIC scores, however, showed improvement in my English. In September of 2000 I scored a 635. I jumped to a 765 in late October of the same year. Later, in March of 2001, I improved even more with a score of 795. I was considered an AA on the TOEIC scale and Level Data sheet – proficient in English! Of course, I had a long way to go to 990, their top score, with an AAA rating level.

I found myself in a familiar setting at ALA – the only American in a class of foreigners. But this time it was a multicultural group rather than a homogeneous one. I studied with foreign students from Asia, Africa, South America, and Europe and became friends with many of the students, not only those from Japan. We had some events, like international dinners, where we cooked and shared our ethnic cuisine. I competed in table tennis championship matches with Venezuelans and Koreans. We went sightseeing to places like Chicago or elsewhere, visiting museums, amusement parks, shopping malls, or historical sites. Despite being an

American boy from Indiana, the places I visited with the international students were just as unfamiliar to me as they were to them. I was a foreigner in my own country – even my own state.

Romantic relationships also began at ALA. I was attracted to a Korean girl and then to a Thai girl. With the exception of a Swedish girl that I met at my international high school, I was attracted to dark-haired Asian girls rather than blonds. Maybe it was because I was able to understand them better.

I made friends at ALA with people like Sanda, a Muslim from Cameroon, who I played basketball with at the Butler University campus. Arm, from Thailand, had me over to cook Thai food and play video games with him and other international students from the language academy. I promised him I would come visit when I turned 21 so we could drink together. Unfortunately, as a poor college student, I was never able to make the trip, and we celebrated via social media.

The third guy I ended up spending the most time with was Japanese. Hiroyuki was from Hiroshima. We had the same hobbies, like playing *Magic: The Gathering* and Nintendo games. It was to the detriment of his English language development and to my good fortune that I regularly practiced Japanese during my high school years. Years later, in 2006, I was lucky enough to meet him again in Hiroshima when I visited Mom, who was teaching English in Okayama.

Empathetic to my culture shock, Mom registered me for eighth grade at the Indiana Japanese Language School on Saturdays, where I blended with other Japanese students and had *undokai* [sports day] and other Japanese traditions.

Mom had made a promise to then President Kusuo Hitomi of Shōwa Women's University that prompted my enrollment. I was at their meeting when he presented her with an elegant gold-lacquered Japanese box as a parting gift a few days before she left the university. It had been his father, Enkichi Hitomi, an educator and poet, who had founded the school in 1920. The original school buildings were destroyed in a bombing raid during WWII and the school was later rebuilt in Setagaya ward. Grateful for her university experience and the education that I had received, Mom promised him she would continue my Japanese language education back in America.

The Indiana Japanese Language School principal was more than a little surprised to see me proudly wearing my black school uniform on my first day of school. I felt a sense of belonging clad in that Japanese school attire. I was relieved that the other Japanese students didn't make fun of me. Instead, their reaction was subtle, maybe even with a hint of acknowledgment that said, *He's one of us.* Here I was again, the only American white boy in a Japanese school. Sadly, I wore that black uniform only once after returning to America – for now, I had to go back to American traditions by wearing casual clothes.

At the age of 14, after graduating from the American Language Academy, I enrolled into the International School of Indiana (ISI). Attending this private school was a brand-new experience for me. With the exception of the ALA, where I completed classes in the Intensive English Program, it was unlike any school I'd attended before, filled with multicultural students, many from Europe and South America.

From Bowing to Hugging

One of the biggest shocks I experienced at ISI was all the hugging and kissing. Coming from Japan, where intimate affection is rarely displayed, I was overwhelmed by the sense of touch. *Oh no, here they come again with their greetings. Just act normal! Is this behavior even allowed in school?*

My situation was exacerbated by a bad case of acne that I struggled with for the next four years. Facials, cleansing products, and medicinal ointments were a normal part of my hygiene routine through high school. Other students didn't make a big deal of it – probably because my Japanese mannerisms stood out even more. Every morning, I bowed to my high school peers instead of waving. As most of the international students were originally from overseas, ISI required all students to enroll in an intensive French or Spanish track as part of their educational experience. Despite already being bilingual, I chose Spanish as my language track and slowly adjusted to school life.

I was actually terrified of learning another language because I knew all too well the struggles I'd been through to learn English. I stayed the weakest in English throughout my four years at ISI and failed the Indiana state-mandated standardized test for high school students twice before eventually passing.

I attribute my English improvement not just to teachers and Mom's tutoring but also to my high school friend Adam. Little did I know at the time that he was just as hesitant and excited to meet me as I was to meet him. He remembers encountering me in a school hallway on my first day at ISI.

"Are you Casey?" he asked, stuttering awkwardly. He had an interest in all things Japanese like anime and manga and had heard about me.

"Yes, I'm K C," I said, hoping that the syllables of my name were clearly enunciated. As Adam approached, I noticed immediately that he wasn't put off by my severe acne.

He was quick to respond. "Hello, Casey. I'm Adam. Our mothers have met and my mother told me to meet you."

I could sense he was embarrassed about that introduction. I mentioned I hadn't been told that our moms had met. He later admitted to me that he regretted such an awkward first meeting. But the friendship Adam showed me during my cultural adaptation to the American high school system was grounding. We were both 14 when we met on that first day of school. Later, at 16, I remember him picking me up for school in his 1990 Blue Buick Reatta on many mornings, a treat since I didn't have a car of my own. Adam and I hung out together throughout this period, sharing our American and Japanese interests. It's making friends, more than anything else, that eases culture shock.

I was sitting in Spanish class when news of the World Trade Center attack broke in September 2001. We spent the rest of the class glued to the television as the second airplane struck the towers. Our school went into lockdown. All of us were in shock and full of sadness at what had taken place. In October of 2001, just after 9/11, I was asked by Ruth Van Reken to participate in the fourth Annual Conference of Families in Global Transition in Indianapolis. This was the first time I'd heard the term 'Third Culture Kid' (TCK). The conference was a forum for members of internationally mobile corporate, military, diplomatic, and missionary families to gather with those who assisted them, including human resource personnel, relocation experts, educators, and counselors. Like this memoir, my presentation reflected on my experiences while living in Japan. Soon after, I was featured in *Kaigai Shijo Kyoiku*, a publication of the Japan Overseas Educational Services, which shared my struggles to adapt – as outlined in my presentation.[4]

The final adventure of my high school life involved out-of-state school trips to a couple of remote locations, one of which I never dreamed I would visit: Costa Rica. The purpose of our trip was to do community service at a local orphanage. After landing, we got on a bus where we were met by some of the local orphanage students. I was swept off my feet by a Latina beauty who was there to escort us. We held eye contact for a few moments. I was praying I'd see her again during my two-week stay in Costa Rica.

The lodging unit I stayed in was the only area with a television. Most nights, students from the school gathered to watch *Los Simpson* (The Simpsons). This is where I first had the chance to talk to Elsie, the girl on the bus who had caught my eye. She was an orphan from El Salvador. We spent time together shopping as a group in San José and smelling the sulfur vapor at Crater Diego de la Haya. We played soccer and walked around town with other kids from the orphanage. I felt my exposure to other countries and cultures was expanding. But my fondest memory was Elsie. With the help of the Spanish teacher, I wrote her a poem to tell her how I felt. As a parting gift, she spent the last night teaching me a South American folk dance under the stars.

I was scolded a few times after returning to Indiana for racking up long-distance phone bills with Elsie. I guess learning Spanish had provided some romantic dividends, but more importantly, thriving in a different environment helped me break out of my shell and deal with my reverse culture shock. Like an athlete training in the mountains, I came back to the U.S. more confident than ever in who I was becoming.

A Tale of Two High Schools

March 2005 was the end of my formal Japanese education when I graduated at the age of 19. Four Japanese diplomas carefully rolled into their tall leather-textured cases decorated my bookshelf, one from kindergarten (Tokyo), one from elementary school (Kanazawa), one from Japanese Middle School (Indiana), and one from Japanese High School (Indiana). Displayed next to those a little later was my American High School diploma, which I received from the International School of Indiana in May of that year.

It was strange not having to wake up early on Saturdays anymore; doing so had been a regular routine since my arrival in Indiana in April of 2000. I certainly did not miss having to do all of the extra homework, though! Despite my struggles, I managed to have a typical American high school experience. I was a member of the varsity basketball team, playing center forward. I played Dungeons & Dragons after school with friends. I went to house parties with my classmates and did community service when I broke the rules. Although my school never found out, the worst thing I did during my high school years was shoplifting from a large local department store.

It was around the holidays of 2004, and I thought if I took a few packages of *Magic: The Gathering* card packs and sold them, I could make some money to purchase Christmas gifts for my family. The security cameras caught me. As I was about to walk out of the store with Mom, a couple of the security officers escorted me to a private room. They asked me to empty my pockets. The store personnel told me that since the amount was over $100, I would need to spend a night in juvenile jail. Later I found out Wade had quietly asked the store manager to give me the rough treatment so I would learn a valuable lesson. Indeed, I never forgot the experience. The police officers handcuffed me, walked me outside in front of the store, and put me in the small metal compartment of a paddy wagon, a police van used for transporting wrongdoers. Mom was an emotional wreck for the duration of the ordeal. I was bunked with another boy who had spat in his mother's face, among other dirty deeds he bragged about. My parents came to pick me up before daybreak. However, the real punishment came later as I was required by the state to serve over 100 hours of community service at a local food bank warehouse.

No matter the reason, my theft was a crime. Along with good friends I had made at ISI, I'd also made a few questionable ones. I'd watched these friends shoplifting on occasions and was stunned at how easily they pulled it off. I was convinced I could do the same. It was like a rite of passage into a new friend group, perhaps symptomatic of my reverse culture shock. I'd forgotten the memory of Mom's purse at the bus stop in Japan and the moral integrity of the Japanese people. These were risks I would never have otherwise taken.

Because the student population of ISI was small due to it being a new school, I got to experience a high school prom twice as the school combined several grades for the event. Attending a high school prom is a special experience. I asked Mae, a Thai girl who I'd met at the American Language Academy, to be my prom date. We dated for most of my time in high school. In fact, my first job was working at a Thai restaurant as a dishwasher. Mae worked there as a part-time waitress and got me hired. She was eight years older than me and a graduate student studying International Relations; my parents and other relatives were not keen on the age gap since I was still an underage minor in high school. Mae looked like a young teenager, despite her years. Both of us identified with our Asian upbringing and found commonality in our identity struggles living in the Midwest of the United States. We parted ways at the airport as I headed off to college in Hawai'i, and she returned to Thailand. I appreciated having someone to share so much with during those years I reacquainted myself with Western culture.

It was customary for ISI to feature an International Festival on a given day of the school year where students dressed up and represented a certain nation. Since most students were from European and South American countries, I was the lone representative for Japan. I proudly wore a traditional cotton *yukata* [a man's long robe] and *geta* [wooden slippers] while carrying the Japanese flag. It was like saluting an old friend. Compared to previous schools, public or private, the students at ISI were welcoming of my unique background. My Japanese habits, like bowing, were something they affectionately made fun of, but understood. Since most students came from different backgrounds, we found humor in each other's cultures and teased each other in a playful way.

Cosmic Crossroads

I've been amazed by space and the stars since the age of eight. In one of our adventures, Dad and I joined a group of astronomers on a star-gazing trip into the mountains of California. I was amazed at the mystery around me and still remember the details, like how they used a 40–50 cm diameter reflecting telescope. I was fascinated by the star Vega for its hint of bright blue. To this day, I love looking at the night sky wherever I am in this world.

In my sophomore year of high school, I entered the physics course and chose it as one of my higher-level IB (International Baccalaureate) subjects for junior and senior year. Everything I learned about physics just seemed to make sense. Some topics were difficult to understand and required study time to comprehend, but I loved the process.

It was also in my sophomore year that several scientists from Eli Lilly and Company, where Wade worked, came to hear our student presentations at a science fair held at my school. I won a first-place award with my presentation on melting ice. The topic had to be something related to helping the environment. Since Indiana had experienced a problem with icy roads after a severe and snowy winter, I tested several substances to determine what melts ice the fastest and what keeps it melted the longest, such as iodized salt, rock salt, and so on. I was certain that I wanted to concentrate on science and to study astrophysics.

I dreamed of figuring out how black holes defy space and time and how they can reveal more information about gravity. I dreamed of solving problems associated with prolonged space missions. I dreamed of someday going into space and boarding the International Space Station, as if my teenage struggles had given me the confidence to go into a radically different kind of culture shock all over again. When deciding on a college major and where to study, my Uncle David encouraged me to stay in Indiana, where I'd be a big fish in a little pond. However, I chose to be a small fish in a big pond and attend the University of Hawai'i at Hilo, where I chose astronomy as my major. With a solid foundation in both American and Japanese culture, I set off for the crossroads of the Pacific, Hawai'i, to find my way as an adult TCK.

NOTES

1   Hooper, K. L. (2000, December 11). Mixed blessings for third-culture kids. *The Indianapolis Star*, A1, A8.

2   Pollock, D. C., & Van Reken, R. E. (1999). *The Third Culture Kid Experience: Growing Up Among Worlds.* Nicholas Brealey Publishing.

3   In an alphabetic language like English, children learn the phonetic value of letters, letter groups, and syllables. Memorizing pictures demands different brain functioning. In fact, researchers have discovered that an individual's mother tongue affects how a person processes mathematical problems. An article by NBC News

(https://www.nbcnews.com/id/wbna13560741) says that native English speakers and people who learn Chinese as a first language use different parts of the brain when using Arabic numerals. Although Arabic numerals are also used in Japan and China, both countries use Chinese characters to represent numerical values. It's more common to see Arabic numerals used in horizontal writing, while Chinese characters are used in vertical writing. That difference "may mean that Chinese speakers perform problems in a different manner than do English speakers." This may explain why Asians and Westerners differ in thought patterns due to their use of a "brain region involved in the processing of visual information."

4   Kaigai Shijo Kyoiku Shinko Zaidan. (n.d.). *Introduction to Japan Overseas Educational Services.* Japan Overseas Educational Services. https://www.joes.or.jp/introduction

QR code for
Chapter Five
photographs

CULTURAL SYNOPSIS

CHAPTER SIX
Adapting as a TCK

This chapter represents the fourth stage of culture shock, known as the adaptation stage. During my college experience in Hawai'i, halfway between Asia and America, I began to adapt to my cultural identity as a TCK.

- Imagine that a chameleon is also in a coloration crisis. My college days felt like I was constantly struggling to adapt, unsure whether to show the Red Sun of Japan or the Star-Spangled Banner to fit my new American surroundings.

- The University of Hawai'i at Hilo was a landscape that was both familiar and unfamiliar. I recognized the Hawai'i I'd known on O'ahu island with its tropical flora, fauna, and aqua-hued ocean – yet the vast nature of Hawai'i island was overwhelming for a kid who'd grown up a block away from school in the world's most populated city.

- When I transferred in the spring of 2007 to the main University of Hawai'i (UH) campus in Honolulu, it was only natural that I would become a member of the

International Student Association (ISA) on the UH-Moana campus. After all, I considered myself an international student and felt most comfortable among the multicultural members.

- My time with the ISA grounded me in my sense of self. I realized I could wear my different colors at different moments without ever abandoning my own identity.

- The people at ISA became my closest friends, whom I never saw as foreign at all.

- My American shell made me comfortable with the mic, but my Japanese spirit gave me empathy so I could relate to and interact with others.

- It's always the intercultural people in my life who knock me out of my perspective – trips to see friends, or thinking about people like Wade, who taught me to believe that it's every person's duty to improve the world in their own way and leave something behind that can help others.

- I'd graduated from university and landed a job in business, but I became worried about whether it really was the place for me.

ADAPTING AS A TCK
(2005-2013)

No Place to Rest

A chameleon is an unwelcome pest in Hawai'i that alters the native ecosystem, and that's just how I felt. Imagine that a chameleon is also in a coloration crisis. My college days felt like I was constantly struggling to adapt, unsure whether to show the Red Sun of Japan or the Star-Spangled Banner to fit my new American surroundings. I didn't know how to adapt at all. The University of Hawai'i at Hilo was a landscape that was both familiar and unfamiliar. I recognized the Hawai'i I'd known on O'ahu island with its tropical flora, fauna, and aqua-hued ocean ~ yet the vast nature of Hawai'i island was overwhelming for a kid who'd grown up a block away from school in the world's most populated city. Even within the cultural context of Hawai'i, Honolulu, the

101

Hawaiian capital on Oʻahu, seemed worlds apart from the tiny town of Hilo on the northeastern side of the Big Island.[1] I'd chosen astronomy as my major, with coursework that was impossible to finish in the inadequate 24 hours of a day. But it was new intercultural friendships at school and cultural battles in dormitory life that posed the biggest challenge of all.

I made a few friends from the Micronesian nations of Palau, Guam, the Republic of the Marshall Islands (RMI), the Northern Mariana Islands, and the Federated States of Micronesia (FSM).[2] One of my Micronesian classmates from the state of Chuuk, formerly known as Truk, wore a colorful embroidered skirt to class that contrasted with the jeans and shorts of her peers. Micronesians were another group who came to Hawaiʻi to work in the plantations in the late 1800s and intermixed with various local ethnicities. A steady stream of immigrants began pouring into Hawaiʻi from the 1980s for educational and employment opportunities and for medical services.[3]

Aside from my Micronesian friends, my first roommate at UH-Hilo was a white guy, like me on the surface. Unfortunately, Jimmy's passion for partying and, more significantly, growing and smoking weed, jeopardized my college goals. When I was trying to sleep, he'd wake me up and shout: "It's party time!" It wasn't long before we received our first warning for having alcohol in the dorm. (In Japan, where college campuses are similarly alcohol-free zones, the punishment for breaking the rules is more severe: any student caught having alcohol in the dorm is likely to get thrown out.) Soon after, Jimmy was caught growing weed. Since I was his roommate, I got into trouble. Realizing that I was on my way to expulsion, I had to request a change of roommates.

My next roommate was a Korean guy called Hoyun – a strict, older-brother figure. He would order me to sit on the floor while eating spicy Korean ramen and *kimchi* [Korean salted and fermented vegetables] that his mother had sent him. The smell of our mini fridge was intense. I had to drink *soju* [a Korean alcoholic beverage drunk neat] and play a game called Go-Stop.[4] It used the same playing cards from a Japanese game called *hanafuda* I'd learned to play in Kanazawa with our next-door neighbor, an older woman I called *o-bāchan* or 'grandma.' I never played *hanafuda* to win with *o-bāchan*, but her gentle and detailed instruction over flower-patterned cups of black tea meant I stood a chance against Hoyun.

It was through Hoyun that I met and became part of a larger Korean group on campus. The language structure of Japanese and Korean are identical, and I found the thought process to be similar. Compared to learning Spanish, or even English and Japanese for that matter, learning Korean made sense to me. At last, all I needed to fit in was a bit of vocabulary! In terms of mannerisms, I saw Korean people as being more assertive than the Japanese. I realized I could just act Japanese, while at the same time flaunting some of my American colors. During my first year I was eating Korean food, going to Korean church on the weekend, and becoming interested in Korean girls. I even had a Korean girlfriend.

Academically speaking, I was doing badly. I got a 1.2 out of 4 on my Grade Point Average. In a heart-to-heart phone conversation with Dad one day, he asked, "Do you want to come home and flip burgers at a fast-food restaurant for the rest of your life?"

"No!" I shouted back at him. And I thought, *This is a real wake-up call.*

"Well, if not, you'd better pull it together," said Dad – with love, but sternly.

After that call, I changed roommates again and I turned my grades around. Fortunately, one of my astronomy professors noticed my mixed identity and got me a room in a shared house with some Japanese astrophysicists from Tokyo University. I gave up living with roommates and moved out of the university dorms altogether. My new living space was the size of a walk-in closet. But since my services as a translator/interpreter got me the room rent-free, I was able to save some money. The extra freedom let me spend a lot of time atop Mauna Kea, the world's tallest mountain at 10,205 meters from base to peak.[5] During that time, I volunteered as an astronomy tour guide for people who were visiting the mountain; I became less of an astrophysicist and more of a Japanese interpreter, translator, and overall errand boy.

It was valuable to see firsthand the daily life of an astrophysicist. But although I was interested in the subject matter, I didn't want to work on one of the earth's highest and most isolated points alone in front of a computer tweaking data. Observing the changing cosmos was a lonely and complex pursuit, especially when I was searching for my own identity here on earth. I needed a different path. Without knowing it at first, I came across that path through the chores I had to do to keep living rent-free with the Japanese astrophysicists.

In addition to being an errand boy for the Japanese astrophysicists, I took charge of dealing with their business and financial matters in Hawai'i, making sure the rent and utility bills were paid. Also, each astrophysicist gave me a list of foods they wanted. The grocery store was a 40-minute walk downhill from the house, so I zoomed down on my bicycle and walked back up with sacks of food dangling from the handlebars. I was always buying ingredients for Japanese curry – beef, potatoes, carrots, onions, and curry roux. I had some more niche requests as well, like dried cuttlefish, which they loved snacking on. My bilingual ability, coupled with my growing interest in managing finances, soon catapulted me to the island of O'ahu, where I sought a double major in International Business and Finance at the Shidler College of Business – newly named in 2006 after its alumnus J. Shidler – on the University of Hawai'i at Manoa campus on O'ahu. I really thought that business would be the place for me. I liked managing money and had confidence from dealing with the finances of the Japanese scientists. By the time I graduated from UH-Manoa, I'd earned a cumulative 3.2 Grade Point Average with a 3.6 for my major. It was a massive achievement for someone who started his first semester with a D average and nearly got kicked out for growing pot.

That second year in Hilo was so much better socially too. I became friends with Naoki (an older student from Tokyo), Keith (a friend from Hong Kong who would later become a housemate in Honolulu), and Koji (a friend from Ehime, Japan). Naoki and Koji were peers who I could speak to in Japanese while we all navigated this new culture of America. College life was in full swing. My knack for bartering translation services also worked out with Naoki: he'd invite me over to his place to help with his English studies in exchange for dinner. With limited spending money, I was mainly surviving on a diet of peanut butter/jelly sandwiches and instant ramen with spam – a poor college student's homage to my respective culinary homelands. Having an opportunity to eat proper food was a real treat. If you've never been on a college diet, it might be hard to imagine the motivation a steak dinner at Naoki's gave me to work through the evening. Again, my skills were giving me a free ride.

Naoki was fashionable and debonair. He worked in the airline industry, spoke Italian and Thai (as well as Japanese and English), adorned himself with high-end accessories, and spoke confidently on numerous subjects – all things that awed an impressionable young college kid. But he was also strict. I remember once snacking on some potato chips after dinner while working on his essay. He scolded me for placing my greasy fingers on his computer keyboard. I respected Naoki as an older mentor and positive figure and probably the first person I'd seen who could straddle wildly different cultures with absolute confidence. He held a broad view of the world and I envied his ability to adapt easily. Somewhere in me, the chameleon was starting to recognize its truer calling.

Finding Friends

When I transferred in the spring of 2007 to the main University of Hawai'i (UH) campus in Honolulu, it was only natural that I would become a member of the International Student Association (ISA) on the UH-Moana campus. After all, I considered myself an international student and felt most comfortable among the multicultural members. Involvement in the organization led to three consecutive leadership roles, first as vice president in 2008, then president in 2009, and finally, treasurer in 2010. My academic goals and leadership skills were profoundly influenced by long-time advisors June and Linda, who both held the position of Director of International Student Services. Through their guidance over the years, I was able to have a more positive college experience. There is an interesting link to U.S. history at the ISA. In 1959, at the age of 23, Barack Obama's father became an exchange student to UH-Manoa from Kenya. Barack Obama Sr. helped to found the ISA and became its first president. His studies at UH-Manoa also led to his meeting former President Obama's mother, Stanley Ann Dunham.[6]

My participation at the ISA provided a lot of insight into my identity crises. Unsurprisingly, I found that most Japanese students usually isolated themselves into a homogeneous group, speaking their native language and, generally, not interacting so much with others. I noticed that in meetings they tended to shy away from voicing their opinions and, at times, could even appear arrogant and anti-social in a mixed group. As a leader in the ISA, I was sometimes annoyed at their behavior and their lack of interaction with other, non-Japanese students. My connection with Japanese culture made it even harder for me to accept. Perhaps, as president, I felt a sense of responsibility to ensure everyone paid attention during the meeting. Plus, since Japanese culture was one I was familiar with, I may have been more critical about their behavior and expected more of them. When I was trying to organize an event, it was difficult to get the Japanese students, those whom I identified with most, to take any initiative. Remember the nail that sticks up gets pounded? The Japanese students found that existing within a group offered a safe haven, which was better than sticking out by sharing opinions that might be shot down.

My time with the ISA grounded me in my sense of self. I realized I could wear my different colors at different moments without ever abandoning my own identity. When it came to organizing activities or having social events, I was confident in my ability to bring everyone together. As the ISA president, I was perfectly happy standing in front of an audience with a mic in hand, connecting with all the new faces and welcoming them into the organization.

One time, we organized an overnight beach retreat and camped along the forest line of a local beach. Over that long weekend, with my megaphone in hand, I got to order members around when it came to things like cooking meals. My American shell made me comfortable with the mic, but my Japanese spirit gave me empathy so I could relate to and interact with others.

It's funny that most of my friends were international students from Asia who came to the University of Hawai'i to study English and seek higher education and work. I guess I wasn't that different from them: I too had come to Hawai'i from Asia and struggled with English at first. During my time at UH, I hung out with students from Japan, China, Vietnam, Korea, Taiwan, and other Asian nations. I spent time with Tony, a friend from Guam. During college we'd hang out with other international students, go extreme ironing,[7] or grill some steaks over hot charcoal and crack open some cold beers. We organized ISA activities like beach BBQs on the North Shore,[8] new student welcome and orientation events, fundraising for Chinese earthquake victims, and the annual UH-Manoa International Festival. The people at ISA became my closest friends; I never saw them as foreign at all.

By college graduation in May 2010, I'd built strong friendships. A former Vietnamese study partner, Ti, relocated to New York and now lives in Nova Scotia. A Korean friend, Hyeonjo, went back to Seoul and then returned to UH-Manoa to study for a Ph.D. Corrie, a girl from mainland China I met during college, used her graduate degree in accounting to pursue entrepreneurial ventures. Two brothers from China, Yubin and Libin, were also close friends who made an impression on me – so much so that I later asked Yubin to be the master of ceremonies at my wedding. I asked Jonathan, another close friend from Taiwan, to be my best man. As students, Jonathan and I had spent countless early mornings delivering the University of Hawai'i student newspaper *Ka Leo* to about 70 locations around Honolulu. The early-hours job and the responsibility it demanded created a special bond between us. Yosapon, or 'Pon,' is a Thai friend who lives in Honolulu and who officiated at my wedding ceremony as the minister. Pon and another close friend, Yoji, who is Japanese with Chilean roots, rented a house with me for three years in Kaimuki, a quaint residential neighborhood in Honolulu. I was also Yoji's best man at his Hawai'i wedding.

All of us have fond memories of these few years living together. I often went spearfishing with Yoji and a local friend, Gima. Later, all three of us opened up a bartending business together called Shaka Mixers. We became licensed bartenders, obtained a General Excise Tax license, and tried to build the company through web marketing and word of mouth. I remember our weekly business meetings, pouring beer and concocting new ideas to expand our services. We'd hang a large white sheet across the living room and use a projector to share information and do research together. I admit that most of our time together was spent drinking our own cocktail mixes rather than making any significant sales. We were serious about our venture, but as fledgling entrepreneurs, we got distracted by our happy hours. We got a few gigs before calling it quits as our day jobs got more challenging. It was during this time that I also challenged myself by studying for the LSAT (Law School Admission Test). With my finance background, I thought I might do well in international law. I missed getting into law school by a couple of points and never tried again. Friends had become more important to me than books.

Moms Are Always Right

A few of us were lucky enough to get jobs in Hawai'i after graduation in 2010. One friend found work at a Japanese trading company, while I started my career underwriting mortgages for a mainland company with a local office in Honolulu. I was probably the only hire who ever came down with a bad case of adult chickenpox during the required two-week corporate training in California – no doubt a result of my young transpacific upbringing.[9] [10] Working at that company taught me a lot about the home financing process and about mortgages and loans. It paid well, although I got disillusioned with the pressure of achieving quotas every day and minimizing my error rate. I'd graduated from university and landed a job in business, but I became worried about whether it really was the place for me. To add to the worry was the stress of not wanting to lose my job.

In 2008, two years before I graduated from UH-Manoa, Mom and Wade had relocated from Indiana to Hawai'i. Mom had started a new teaching career in workforce development for the City and County of Honolulu after 20 years of working at universities. Wade had recently conquered stage 3 colon cancer after a colon operation and a year of chemotherapy and radiation. True to his character – and his high tolerance for pain – he told me how he woke up after his surgery, unfastened his intravenous (IV) tube, dressed himself, commandeered a wheelchair, slipped past the nurse's station, and took the elevator down to the first floor of the hospital to buy a coffee.[11] In my mind, he seemed invincible. If Wade could do that, how hard could it be to look for a better job?

Lucky for me, my first full-time job, underwriting mortgages, was only a 10-minute walk when I moved in with Mom and Wade in their bamboo-floored Honolulu condo. The two-bedroom second-floor unit provided just enough room for the three of us, and each bedroom had its own bath and shower. I spent a lot of time taking oatmeal baths there when I had chickenpox.

It was around 2012 that I began complaining to Mom about my work.

"Mom, you remember how I had to walk over an hour to

school in Nakajo for 5th grade?" I said, hunching my shoulders at the breakfast table.

"Yes, of course, honey. Why?" she asked, pausing before she opened the dishwasher.

"Well, I'm starting to hate this 10-minute walk more than that."

"What? Don't you like your job? Isn't it what you studied in school?"

"Uh-huh... but I don't know if it's the right fit. I don't even go to the restroom until lunch in case I hurt my daily quota. I wasn't expecting to become a robot. And I'm not even using my Japanese."

"Casey, if you're unhappy with the situation, then do something about it," Mom said, clattering away as she put the clean dishes back in their places. "You have so much to offer, just look at your amazing background."

"Not at this job," I said, and I trudged to the fridge to find something sweet.

I appreciated her encouragement. Like my grandpa, Mom was defined by her times. She grew up during the civil rights movement and remembers the discriminatory signs, the protest marches, and the forced integration when African-American teens were bussed to her high school in the late 60s. The Vietnam War was still going on in 1972, and the military draft had had an impact on many of the male students at her high school. Convinced that women should also serve their country, Mom enlisted in the Air Force. Her boyfriend at the time, Charles (Chuck), who she'd known since first grade, had already signed up. He enlisted in the Air Force, and shortly after she did too. Joining the WAF (Women in the Air Force) opened my mother's eyes to racial injustice and gender inequality. It wasn't until 1976 that the WAF was ended and women were allowed into the Air Force as equal members.[12] She told me that during her technical training she was sexually assaulted by an instructor. At that time, there were no avenues for a female airman to report abuse. She also told me a story about being refused service at a local restaurant in Biloxi, Mississippi, where she'd gone with a black friend from the Air Force.

More than anything, it was Mom's willingness to take risks that helped me to adjust and cope with my cross-cultural journey. She'd never been on an airplane during the first 19 years of her life – until she joined the military. Enlisting gave her a chance to fulfill her desire to travel and see the world. After basic training at Lackland Air Force Base in San Antonio, Texas, and technical training as an Administrative Specialist at Keesler Air Force Base in Biloxi, Mississippi, she was given orders to her first duty station at RAF Upper Heyford, England. Her first marriage was to a naturalized American citizen, born in Canada, who she met while stationed there. Later, they both went to college, first in California and then in Minnesota. In 1977 they volunteered to serve as short-term missionaries in Eastern Europe, where they smuggled Bibles, Christian literature, medical supplies, and recording equipment into the Iron Curtain countries of Romania, Czechoslovakia, and former Yugoslavia. Her stories about carefully hiding contraband material, deciphering coded information, entering no-man's-land, and having their vehicle searched by armed guards is the stuff of spy dramas. I might have had an older sibling from her first marriage, but this relationship proved to be childless. They ended up divorcing in Indiana.

Mom later began a teaching career, and many of her international students would keep in touch or years later track her down for a visit. She was a warm and empathetic teacher, and very hardworking. I remember Mom grading essays late into the night when I was a young boy and then rising early to type up a test or quiz in the pre-dawn shadows. I was aware of the personal and professional battles she'd had to fight to receive such respect from her students. Watching and learning from Mom helped form my TCK identity. To achieve what I really wanted, I would need determination like hers. And I would need to take risks.

A few days after Mom telling me to do something about my uneasiness, I told her and Wade that I was moving out. My college friends Pon and Yoji were looking for a third person to rent a house with them in Kaimuki. I needed to be with my friends again, particularly with a punishing workload under-writing mortgages. I hoped the change of scene would bring back my confidence and help me find the answers to my questions.

Getting Out of the Rat Race

At the rental house in Kaimuki, Pon became my confidante. He was like a priest listening in to my confessions – in fact, he later took an online course so he could act as minister at my wedding. The house was a 1929 vintage wooden structure with a large kitchen and combined living and dining rooms.

Pon's room was in the front and there were two more bedrooms, one for me, which was next to the kitchen at the end of the house, and the middle room that Yoji occupied.

Walking into Pon's room after returning home from work, I grumbled to him about my workday. I sat on his bed and muttered his nickname. "Ponyo," I said, "I'm tired. I don't want to do this job anymore."

He greeted me in his usual friendly way while tapping away at his computer keyboard. "Hahaha, hello there, sir. How's it going?"

I laid down on his messy bed, rolling over onto my side to face a stark white wall. "The pressure of reaching quotas every day and not making mistakes – the routine sucks, Pon," I said. "It's the same thing day after day. Plus, I think I'm not so good at this job."

"Is there a reason why you're still there?" he said, looking up from his keyboard to shoot me a concerned look.

"I'm scared because I have bills to pay."

"Well, you're gonna have to keep working until you find something else you enjoy more."

And I thought, *Yes, but the question is, how long's that gonna be?*

Most people don't know what to do after high school or college, and it's even more confusing for an international student. While most young adults might focus on marriage or their job after leaving school, I felt an urge to get away from it all. Luckily, I had friends I'd met during college who'd moved on (or back) to places like Vietnam, Taiwan, South Korea, Japan, and China. I decided to take some trips, hoping this would help me find the headspace to figure out what I wanted to do. Besides, I'd banked up a nice amount of vacation time at the mortgage company and was more than ready for some time off.

My first trip, with my friends Trung and Minh, began on an overnight train from Hanoi, Vietnam, to Sapa in the northwestern Lào Cai Province. While central Sapa was touristy, all around the city there were bright green terraced rice paddies, carved out of the mountains in wavy configurations. The wind carried the sounds of children's laughter, the chimes of oxen and goat bells, and the scent of rain. The wooden homes had no electricity. In one of them, a local family who ran an eatery cooked us a meal of freshly caught chicken that was fire-roasted, feathers and all, while cocooned in a mud shell. Somewhat earthy in flavor, once you got past the mud shell, the chicken was incredible. We swapped stories with one another, my Vietnamese friends interpreting. I thought to myself, *Delivering numerous laughs in a given day certainly beats achieving quotas in an office.*

My next trip came when a close friend, Jonathan, called to invite me to Taiwan for Chinese Lunar New Year. It was a perfect opportunity to give myself a little more time to escape my problems back home. The streets were all decked out in red and gold, with outdoor stalls serving delicacies like snake soup and fried stinky tofu. The slices of snake in a light herbal broth tasted like something between chicken (typical, I know) and cod. The plate of stinky tofu, on the other hand, had the aroma of rotting cabbage and old socks dipped in rancid eggs. (Actually, that would still be an insult to rancid eggs.) Amazingly, it tasted delicious. Like New Year celebrations the world over, visiting extended family was part of the Chinese New Year experience. I got to wish everyone in Jonathan's family *Gōng Shǐ Fā Tsai*, or 'May you have a prosperous new year!' They all wished me prosperity for the coming year too, something I really needed.[13]

On the plane back from Taiwan I began thinking about prosperity and how my friends had made me happier than the good paychecks at my job. I'd heard people say time and again that money can buy momentary pleasure or eliminate immediate problems but can't bring long-term happiness. Still, it's so easy in America to fall into the trap and lose your way out again. It reminded me of the term *yuimaru*, popular in Okinawa, which references how human interaction enriches and cultivates a positive effect on mind-body balance. Okinawa is considered one of the Blue Zones of the world, where high concentrations of people live past the age of 100.[14] Connection with different people gave me a sense of inner peace, contentment, and self-fulfillment. No doubt growing up with Wade – of Okinawan heritage and who unconsciously demonstrated this concept of *yuimaru* – helped me appreciate that these experiences were from investing in friends and people, wherever they're from. If someone needed their car or lawn mower fixed, Wade was always available to help out. Mom once arrived home to find one of our televisions missing; Wade had gifted it to a family across the street who had several children and whose TV had gone out.

Discipline! was the word I displayed on my social media profiles during that time. After one of my confessions with Pon, I took a whiteboard and started to write out a plan of my life based on a 90-year lifespan – if I'm to be that fortunate! I wrote big tasks I wanted to accomplish by certain ages, like writing a book, earning a graduate degree, and learning how to fly a small airplane. The whiteboard reminded me of the brevity of life and would make me pause for a second to realize that life is, indeed, short and fleeting. Writing life plans along with several to-do lists kept me thinking about living my life to the fullest, about how to stay positive, and ultimately how to enjoy the relationships I have with family and friends.

It's always the intercultural people in my life who knock me out of my perspective – trips to see friends, or thinking about people like Wade, who taught me to believe that it's every person's duty to improve the world in their own way and leave something behind that can help others. So, in the midst of all this soul searching, I thought about how I could channel my life experiences into something meaningful.

It took three years before I quit the mortgage job. And the email couldn't have come from anyone else – from Mom with an advertisement about a position at Hawaii Tokai International College. This time, I was ready to take a risk on a life-changing decision.

NOTES

1 The island of Hawai'i is more popularly known as the 'Big Island' and is also famous for Hawai'i Volcanoes National Park. It is one of the eight main islands that make up the state of Hawai'i. O'ahu is the most populous island, nick-named the 'Gathering Place,' and is home to the state's capital city, Honolulu.

2   The Compact of Free Association (COFA) covers the
Republic of the Marshall Islands (RMI), the Federated
States of Micronesia (FSM), and the Republic of Palau.
Geographically recognized together as Micronesia, each
place is unique in its identifying culture and language.

3   Hawaiʻi is known for its Aloha Spirit, which is about
harboring good thoughts and feelings toward others.
Naturally, it cultivates more acceptance toward racial
difference, but Hawaiʻi is not, as some might think, a
racial utopia. Tensions between island ethnicities,
particularly Hawaiian versus Micronesian, exist in the
realms of employment and government benefits,
environmental stewardship, access to and choice of lethal
weapons (owning firearms is prohibited in Palau and the
FSM), and marine sustainability and practice. The United
States famously exploited regions of Micronesia from 1946
with nuclear testing on Bikini Island, which resulted in
severe radioactive contamination of islands and coastal
seas, with devastating health consequences for inhabitants.

Heine, H. C. (2002). Culturally Responsive Schools for
Micronesian Immigrant Students: *PREL Briefing Paper*.
Pacific Resources for Education and Learning.

Gus-Williams, I., & Hobro, M. E. (2021, May 17). *Hawaiʻi
is not the multicultural paradise some say it is*. National
geographic.
https://www.nationalgeographic.com/culture/article/hawa
ii-not-multicultural-paradise-some-say-it-is

4   Go-stop is a Korean fishing card game played with the same 48-card deck as *hanafuda* (or *Hwatu* in Korean). The colorful cards represent culturally significant scenes of seasonal flowers, animals, and other depictions. The object of the game is to strategically collect numerous pairs and score high points.

5   Tallest mountain. (n.d.). Guinness World Records. Retrieved May 15, 2021, from https://www.guinnessworldrecords.com/world-records/tallest-mountain

6   Obama, B. (2004). *Dreams from my father: A story of race and inheritance.* New York: Three Rivers Press. (p. 9)

7   Extreme ironing is when you take an ironing board, an iron, and a shirt on a hike to ultimately snap a photograph of you ironing the shirt someplace remote and difficult to reach. Naturally, no electricity is involved.

8   Commonly referred to as the 'North Shore,' this popular area of Oʻahu is famous for big wave surfing and a rural lifestyle with quaint shops and restaurants. Change is slow here compared to the south side of the island, and it almost feels like another island when visiting.

9   Japan was the first country to develop a chickenpox vaccine. It was nationally approved for use in 1986, the same year I was born. The U.S. first licensed a chickenpox vaccine in 1995. I may have escaped having the contagious disease as a child due to my young Japanese peers having

already been vaccinated, and so I experienced a more severe version as a young man in my 20s.

10   *What is the history of chickenpox vaccine use in America and other countries?* (n.d.). National Vaccine Information Center. Retrieved July 24, 2021, from https://www.nvic.org/vaccines-and-diseases/chickenpox/vaccine-history.aspx

11   Wade has been in remission for over 10 years. He works full time as a federal contractor in occupational safety.

12   Arce, C., & Dabbs, R. (2020, December 23). *Women in the Air Force: A walk in their boots.* Sixteenth air force (air forces cyber). https://www.aetc.af.mil/News/Article-Display/Article/2459126/women-in-the-air-force-a-walk-in-their-boots/

13   People think they understand a culture, when in fact, they only know the tip of the iceberg. It can seem easy to embrace external and clearly visible elements of a culture, such as its language, cuisine, dress, customs, and celebrations. But beneath all these things lie more in-depth aspects of a culture, like its views of authority, morals surrounding guilt and shame, conception of reality, religious beliefs, and other complicated subjects related to what also brings happiness. Prosperity is really important in China, and the joy of being a TCK is connecting with people who live a life on the other side of the world from you but who look for the same things in life.

14   *The Secret of Okinawan Longevity*. (n.d.). Visit Okinawa. Retrieved June 4, 2021, from https://www.visitokinawa.jp/about-okinawa/blue-zone-okinawa

QR code for
Chapter Six
photographs

CULTURAL SYNOPSIS

CHAPTER SEVEN
Accepting My Destiny

Chapter Seven describes acceptance. Although acceptance is not included as a stage of culture shock in the preface of my book, I have written this chapter to reflect my own experience. It reflects how I have come to terms with my cultural identity moving forward.

- If it was Wade who fulfilled the role of my Asian mentor, then it was my biological dad, Tom, who cemented my Americanness.

- The interview process at Tokai for the International Program Coordinator position was a journey in itself. When I got the phone call and offer of a position, it felt like something had come full circle. There I was, back in the same environment I grew up in.

- I suppose if I've been called an ethnic and cultural egg, with her upbringing in California, my wife Yukiko could be called a banana. Had I not experienced life as a TCK, it's likely we would never have connected like we did.

- In the eight years I've worked for HTIC, I've greeted and waved goodbye to thousands of students. Over the years, I've watched students lose their shyness and expand their view of the world.

- In my mind, a lot of the world's problems come down to a battle between the collective and the individual. It's complicated balancing an individual's freedom of choice with what is best for the greater good.

- Writing my own 3D journey through the stages of culture shock has made me more aware of the identity struggles I suffered growing up. I'm lucky to have emerged as a guide for others at the start of their intercultural journey.

- Although I've accepted my destiny, I still feel I am seeking the final piece of the puzzle.

CHAPTER SEVEN

ACCEPTING MY DESTINY
(2013–2021)

My Old Man

I called Dad to discuss quitting my job and applying for the position at Hawaii Tokai International College.

"Dad, you know how I've been complaining about my job lately?" I said, cooling myself in my Mazda 3's AC. After his previous comment about me working at a fast-food restaurant if I didn't improve my college performance, I was anxious to get his approval.

"Yeeeees," Dad replied with a long-drawn-out pronunciation of the word.

"Well, I finally feel I'm ready to take a leap. I applied for that new job I was telling you about," I said confidently but with a hint of nervousness.

"That's great! I'm proud of you, son," he answered with an upbeat tone and genuine interest.

Dad and I had agreed to have weekly talks over the phone, where he'd usually tell me about his latest business idea. Despite a few strokes of bad luck along the way, he never lost his excitement. And this time, Dad had taken the risk of opening a restaurant in no other place than Costa Rica. While he'd been busy starting a new livelihood on another continent, I'd been worrying about changing jobs on the same island.

It always struck me when visiting Dad that he owned fewer possessions compared to most other adults in my life. He was a minimalist, and fewer possessions allowed him to move freely, reduce maintenance costs, and worry less about leaving places behind. I always felt like I was in a different world when spending time with Dad. Every year during school vacations, I visited him for hiking, skiing, fishing, kayaking, ice skating, and road trips from Lake Tahoe to Indy via the Grand Canyon, or around Oregon, Crater Lake, and the Cascade Mountain Range. I felt American with Dad. He loved having a big yard with a big dog, shopped at Trader Joe's, and listened to old albums on his record player.[1] It was as if my Asian identity was on hold when I was with him. When we were together, he'd re-teach me how to make the perfect omelet, and then we'd sit down to a game of chess on his black-and-green marble chess board.

America was Dad's comfort zone. According to him, to be American was to be outgoing, to speak your mind, and to make your point understood. I knew that the United States ranked 91 out of 100 as the top-rated nation for individualism on Hofstede's 6 Dimensions Model of National Cultures.[2] Dad's American psyche supported this statistic. That being said, he was always adamant about protecting democracy in the United States, and he wrote to Oregon state senator Ron Wyden to ask for tighter gun regulations. Despite our trips to the outdoors, my dad never took me to shoot guns for fun or to hunt animals. He's also never owned a gun.

If it was Wade who fulfilled the role of my Asian mentor, then it was my biological dad, Tom, who cemented my Americanness. He taught me never to give up, to stand on my feet, and to appreciate excellence over mediocrity. He'd always insist: "Don't buy junk! You often get what you pay for. If you're going to spend money on something, get a quality product that's going to last a long time. You'll appreciate it more and get a longer life out of the product."[3]

Dad was also the one to tell me: "When you shake someone's hand, your grip needs to be firm and you need to look them in the eye. It signifies confidence and your presence, while acknowledging them as an individual. That's how we do it here."

"Yes, Dad," I said at the time, and rather than bowing, as was my habit, I looked him straight in the eye.[4]

During our early years living in Japan, Dad had worked hard to make a life for us. He had a degree in Restaurant/Hotel Institute Management from Purdue University and was innovative in finding work for himself. He developed a catering business within the confines of our foreign-teacher-occupied apartment building. Every day he offered two different dishes for residents to choose from in the morning, and when they returned home that evening, Dad would have their meals waiting for them. He'd carefully shop at the local Japanese markets, often with a Japanese/English dictionary, and spend his day cooking in the kitchen until it was time to deliver his orders to each teacher's doorstep. The service was very much welcomed.

Sometimes I helped Dad on his deliveries, distributing fish dishes like salmon or swordfish, beef stew with French bread and salad, or his popular chicken marsala. Later, he found hospitality positions at the Tokyo American Club and the New Sanno Hotel and caught the train into central Tokyo. If anyone was going to be supportive of me trying out a new career idea, it was my dad.

A Career in Academia

The interview process at Tokai for the International Program Coordinator position was a journey in itself. Before being offered the job, I had to undergo two rounds of interviews. I met both the group I would be working with and the executive committee. I also had to take a Japanese language proficiency exam. On my third visit, I sat alone at the Chancellor's dark oak table on the ninth floor overlooking Waikiki and the panic set in. My Japanese language skills, especially reading and writing, were rusty, and I remember thinking, *Crap, am I going to fail this?* My future supervisor, Yabe, knocked and entered the office. She was carrying a laptop and a sheet of paper that had the text of a business mail in Japanese with some questions.

"Hi Casey, are you ready?" she asked.

"It's been a little while since I've written Japanese," I said, "but I'll do my best."

"That's fine, just do as much as you can. You'll have 30

minutes to type replies to these questions on the paper using Word on the computer."

"Can I use an online dictionary?" I asked, hoping a smile would do the trick.

"The laptop doesn't have Internet. You'll just have to use the vocabulary you know. It's part of the test. Well, good luck!" she said, and she walked out of the office and closed the door behind her.

My heart sank. I had to summon up all the Japanese I'd learned, otherwise it was back to meeting quotas. After 30 minutes, Yabe returned and took a look at my work. Keeping a blank face, she saved the Word document and left, saying she'd be right back. She returned with the Chancellor and they both sat down and began chit-chatting with me in English and Japanese. I had no idea whether I'd be hired or not and was told I'd be receiving a call from Human Resources within the week. I never saw the actual results of the test, but I must have passed one way or another.

When I got the phone call and offer of a position, it felt like something had come full circle. There I was, back in the same environment I grew up in. Entering college on my first day of work, nostalgic memories of my years among international students came flooding back. It felt familiar. It felt comfortable. As is Japanese tradition, three of us shared my new office space – Yabe the director, me, and another coordinator. The office was located on the southeast corner of the ninth floor, with a killer view of Diamond Head, the Waikiki skyline, and the adjacent aqua-blue sea. Except for a computer and a lucky bamboo plant in a panda-shaped pot, which Mom had given me, my desk was bare. It didn't take long before I buried it with paperwork and other work-related flotsam. I worked at this location for a couple of years until a brand-new campus was completed on the sunny and dry leeward side of Oʻahu. I lost the million-dollar view, but by that time it didn't matter.

Marriage to a Japanese Princess

Muffins first united my wife, Yuki, and me. She was an English-as-a-second-language (ESL) teacher in the College Preparatory Program at Hawaii Tokai International College. I met her at the former HTIC campus in Waikiki before it relocated to the leeward side of the island in 2015, where she liked to bake treats and leave me one in my work mailbox. Channeling my dad's cooking energy, I crafted a combined Rice Krispies and Cocoa Krispies treat to give to her. I guess they were good because she thought I'd bought them at a store – until a few months later when she discovered I'd made them.

I was blessed to find her. Although Yuki was born in Tokyo, she spent her formative years in Los Angeles and is more fluent in English than I am in Japanese. A mirror reflection of myself in many ways, she also left her place of birth to live in a foreign country at the age of three. We both share a bilingual, bicultural upbringing and a mutual understanding of American/Japanese history, tradition, and nuance. I suppose if I've been called an ethnic and cultural egg, with her upbringing in California, she could be called a banana. Had I not experienced life as a TCK, it's likely we would never have connected like we did.

We tied our marital knot atop a hill overlooking UH-Manoa on September 8, 2017, in a simple but memorable affair with only a few close friends and family present. It was on the same date a year later that we held a traditional wedding with friends and family joining us from all over the world. We held an outdoor ceremony at The Bayer Estate, a charming vintage seaside venue on the East side of Honolulu known for being a filming site for the Hawaii Five-0 series. As guests arrived, Yoji and Gima donned the Shaka Mixer's aprons and performed one last gig as bartenders. My college friend from Taiwan, Jonathan, was my best man, while Pon officiated as our minister. Our ring bearer was The Bayer Estate property owner's mixed Golden-Labrador, Yogi, who did a fine job carrying out his duty, albeit with two intense training sessions prior to the big day.

Following the wedding, all the guests transitioned to the Halekulani Hotel in Waikiki, where we dined and danced. Yubin, my friend from China, did an outstanding job as our Master of Ceremony. At the end of the reception, we filmed a live music video beginning with *Lucky* by Jason Mraz, which we sang to each other before a medley of popular dance songs. Balloons, quirky sunglasses, party top hats, feather boas, and Mardi Gras beads were used by guests as they hit the dance floor to make a video of our wedding.[5]

What a breathtaking bride Yuki was, her beauty and delicate features enhanced by her backless, spaghetti strap floor-length gown. Auntie Seiko, Wade's sister-in-law and a professional wedding planner, and Jay, Yuki's colleague and bridesmaid, accompanied her along with my mom to choose the perfect dress. I remember them saying she chose the last dress she tried on, and she'd tried on over a dozen. The gown was detailed with exquisite lace and decorated with what resembled tiny stars sparkling on the full skirt. She looked amazing on the dance floor, so much so that I had to ask myself what good had I done in my life to deserve this lady.

Yuki looked like a princess, and based on her Japanese ancestry she isn't far off being one. Yuki's grandfather on her mother's side was a great-grandson of the last Japanese shogun, 徳川 慶喜, or Tokugawa Yoshinobu. I married a girl whose lineage comes from royal ancestors – princes, barons, and counts. A few of her relatives on both her father and mother's side had been important politicians, industrialists, and philanthropists of the Japanese aristocracy. These people had held significant roles in society and in the making of modern Japan.

Yuki's heritage, combined with her academic success, was intimidating and I wanted to be good enough for her and her family. I was aware that Yuki's family might be concerned about the educational gap once she obtained her doctoral degree. Generally, families in Japan worry about whether their child's education level is suitably matched with a potential partner. Both Yuki and her father encouraged me to pursue my graduate degree. I lacked some confidence. I was far from the best student and certainly wasn't as studious as she was. Could I manage a full-time job *and* coursework?

Harnessing My Superpower

In the eight years I've worked for HTIC, I've greeted and waved goodbye to thousands of students. Decorating the bulletin board next to my desk is a collection of *shikishi* (square bits of white cardboard) with pictures and thank you messages from students.[6] As a student, I received similar white cardboard messages from my Japanese classmates. The only difference was that, back then, the messages were written to say farewell; these were to say thank you. Many of the HTIC students who wrote to me have gone on to further studies abroad. One of the messages read, "I never thought I would have done this. Thank you, Casey!" Another student wrote, "Thank you for this experience! It was my first time leaving Japan. I want to travel to more new places."

Over the years, I've watched students lose their shyness and expand their view of the world. These students – who come not only from Japan but from other countries too – stay at our campus for anywhere between a week and two months. I serve a variety of educational levels ranging from elementary to graduate students. My job is to ensure their stay in Hawai'i is positive, meaningful, and educational. In short, it has to be inspiring. Planning their curriculum and coordinating with outside vendors is my primary responsibility. I've developed a network of island educational institutions, teachers and professors, companies, and cultural practitioners who can be counted on to share their knowledge and wisdom with the students. While my position demands a substantial number of administrative tasks and paperwork, and some teaching, the most rewarding part comes from seeing the students enjoy themselves during the program, especially when they go on educational excursions around the island – a classroom without walls.

Imagine this scenario. It's 8:00 am Saturday morning and the bright Hawaiian sun is beaming down across the school campus. A prearranged rented yellow school bus rolls up in front of the campus flagpoles. Addressing the student's high anticipation, I greet them in English with, "Good morning! It's a great day for a trip around the island. Are you guys excited?"

In unison I hear, "Yes, *sensei*. We are ready for beach!"

"That's great. Be sure to get a bottle of water before you get on the bus. It's going to be hot today," I warn them.

"Yes, I have," some respond. As the students board the bus, I count them to make sure no one is still snoozing in their dorm room.

"Attention, everyone! Our first stop today will be Makapu'u Lighthouse, where we will take a short hike. You'll enjoy the magnificent view of Rabbit Island and the ocean scenery. After that, we'll stop by Halona Blowhole, where you can see a rare wonder of nature. Ancient lava tubes will shoot salty sea water up to 30 feet high! Later, we'll have a local *bento* lunch at Kailua Beach. Finally, we'll check out the Pali Lookout on our way back. Are you ready!?"

A chorus of "We're ready" resounds in my ears while one inquisitive student asks me, "What is the Pali Lookout?"

"Well, the Pali is a sacred battle place where King Kamehameha I[7] and his warriors fought the Kalanikūpule," I explain. "They won this battle which united O'ahu under his rule. But, many warriors were killed and fell off the steep cliff. Legend tells us that you can hear the war cries of the warriors' ghosts in the island wind."

"*Kowa* [scary]!" the student says with emotion.

I laugh. "Haha. Don't worry, I'll be there to protect you!"

There have been many memorable events during my time at Tokai. But my most memorable experience was on a Saturday in January 2018 – at 8:07 in the morning, to be precise. I was sitting at my office desk sipping some hot coffee getting ready for a group excursion to Honolulu when, all of a sudden, piercing emergency tones shot out from my phone. I looked down to read the text alert. 'BALLISTIC MISSILE THREAT INBOUND TO HAWAI'I. SEEK IMMEDIATE SHELTER. THIS IS NOT A DRILL.' My heart skipped a beat. *Why, North Korea, why?* I thought to myself. Immediately, I spoke to security personnel and the few staff on campus. Within minutes students were gathered and then escorted into the hallway, which was in the middle of the administrative building and had no windows. Once there, we waited. I spoke with Yuki and Mom, wondering if it would be the last time, unsure what destructive power was rocketing toward us. Yuki was concerned and asked what she should do as she was at home, while Mom was stuck in a supermarket with Wade. Mom was emotional and told me repeatedly that she loved me. Although some students were scared, I comforted them by saying, "It'll be alright. We're deep in the building and I doubt the missile will reach us."

I was not one to panic and be overly emotional. I passed the time by checking my phone for updates and texting Yuki as she sheltered at home in the bathroom. At 8:45, thirty-eight minutes later, another text alert came through. 'THERE IS NO MISSILE THREAT OR DANGER TO THE STATE OF HAWAI'I. REPEAT. FALSE ALARM.' A huge sigh of relief was heard throughout the hallway as the news spread. After making some phone calls, the school bus company was willing to resume operations and dispatched a bus to our campus.

I made the right decision giving up my previous job – even though it was more lucrative and would have given me greater mobility and financial stability. Though the work hours can be just as long at HTIC, I've discovered the real impact I can have on so many others. *Changing lives is a kind of superpower*, I've told myself in moments of revelation – like when I shared a virtual tour of Oʻahu with Japanese students during the pandemic. Not allowed to travel, the students were, nevertheless, still able to experience American and Hawaiian culture by seeing ordinary, everyday island scenes, with live interaction between teachers and students. As soon as I heard a gasp and an excited "Wow, I hope I can go myself one day," I could rest in the satisfaction that I'd put in a good day's work.

Simulating Culture Shock

I was often targeted as an outsider in Japan. I understood how excluding those who are different from you and how only associating with people who are the same as you fuels intercultural conflict. For example, Korean groups attending HTIC were often suspicious of our Japanese students, and vice versa. I began wondering if I could use technology to bring together groups of students with different cultural backgrounds in neutral learning environments. I thought that education through gaming, in particular, could provide more avenues in understanding how to communicate with people with different assumptions, expectations, and jargon.

It was this thinking, as well as being excluded from certain committees at work due to having only a bachelor's degree, that made me decide to continue my education in 2017 and pursue a Master of Education in Learning Design and Technology degree. I was curious to find answers to these four questions:

1 How will technology play a role in the future in peoples' lives?
2 How will technology affect and change the way humans interact?
3 How can we use technology to teach intercultural interaction?
4 How will technology impact industries, like education, so that the industry or in my case the institution, can be better prepared and pointed in the right direction to best serve its student population?

I thought about the difference between 'equality' and 'equity' when it comes to learning. According to the Milken Institute School of Public Health at The George Washington University, "Equality means each individual or group of people is given the same resources or opportunities. Equity recognizes that each person has different circumstances and allocates the exact resources and opportunities needed to reach an equal outcome."[8] This is where technology, or more specifically virtual reality (VR) and virtual worlds (VW), could be used to level the playing field by removing preconceived prejudices. Virtual reality or virtual world environments are simply an alternative place to reality where users can interact and socialize. My interest was in how technology like this could bridge gaps between cultures and, on a wider scale, establish a path to global understanding. But these technologies have also proved capable of bringing together students with a tendency to isolate themselves, or those who find the classroom difficult because of social, anxiety, or health issues.

There's a common phrase in Japanese, *hikikomori*, that refers to people with a tendency to shut themselves in their room and who often stop going to school or work or socializing at all.[9] Using virtual technology, a person could maintain an anonymous profile while engaging in a somewhat social environment. Perhaps, at best, the person could gradually regain the confidence to reenter society. I also believe that with the COVID-19 pandemic a societal reality, creative and innovative online learning has become a critical tool as learners of all ages are required to access computers from home, rather than be present in a classroom.

In the computer simulation I created for my master's project, I wanted participants (American college students planning to study abroad) to learn about culture shock and its stages by navigating a Minecraft virtual world. Initially, users spawned in a suburban American town and were greeted by a signboard introducing them to the simulation (a link to the actual Minecraft simulation is in footnote 6 of the *Introduction*). From this point, users would follow a pink path taking them on a journey to obtain a passport, board a flight, and travel to Japan. Upon arriving, participants would navigate the surroundings to exit the airport, take a bus, and get off in the middle of a metropolis-like city similar to Tokyo.

I took time to include culturally rich representations like Japanese-language billboards, Japanese vending machines, ticketing booths, cherry blossom trees, temples, iconic buildings, convenience stores, logos, and more. Specific examples included Tokyo Tower, a JR train station, an underground department store, a Zen temple, a 7-Eleven convenience store, Olympics 2020 signs, and Japanese company logos. To exit the city, users would then board a subway train that took them to the countryside, where they could learn about traditional customs, like removing one's shoes upon entering a house. The user's final destination in the simulation was a university setting that included a dorm room and other billboards offering cultural facts about the Japanese educational system. The whole simulation was designed to represent the five stages of culture shock:

STAGE 1: HONEYMOON

The first stage represented the honeymoon stage and contained information about what to expect when first arriving in a foreign country. Learners discovered common reactions such as feelings of excitement and the urge to explore new places, food, and customs. Pictures of these types of cultural aspects were included in the area to illustrate the fun new discoveries they might find when coming to Japan.

STAGE 2: CULTURE SHOCK

The second stage, culture shock, taught them about the hardships and difficulties faced when the honeymoon stage wears off. A signboard at the station mentioned how learners can feel frustrated about cultural differences and feel homesick for their native culture. Common symptoms such as depression, anxiety, and feelings of helplessness were also covered. Additionally, a question was asked about what happens when a person fails to overcome the symptoms of culture shock. The answer revealed that individuals can become hostile to host nationals, thus leading to greater difficulty in developing interpersonal relationships with locals.

STAGE 3: ADJUSTMENT

The third stage, adjustment, instructed users on how to overcome the shock stage by encouraging them to seek a deeper understanding of the host culture. Signage included tips on how to cope with differences since learning what to expect beforehand can drastically lower the shock. Some tips suggested establishing a high degree of self-confidence and optimism, accepting that other cultures are not good or bad but simply different, and urging users to seek social support from new friends, faculty members, or counselors at the host institution.

STAGE 4: ADAPTATION

The fourth stage, adaptation, was presented as a goal that learners should strive for. This station informed them what to expect when reaching this stage in their study abroad experience. Travelers discovered that in this stage, the negative symptoms of culture shock will largely disappear, and personal identity will begin to shift to the point where learners may forget that they are from a different country.

STAGE 5: REVERSE CULTURE SHOCK

The last stage, representing reverse culture shock, taught learners about the struggles of leaving the host country and reentering their home country. The signboard here explained that friends and family back home may not be able to comprehend the cross-cultural experiences and will likely expect the traveler to re-adjust quickly. This frustration can lead to a feeling of alienation but is typically short depending on the duration of the study abroad experience. The final station informed learners that the best way to deal with re-entry shock is to remember the experiences they initially had adjusting to the host culture and apply the same mentality. Students come away learning that extended study abroad experiences can help them feel enlightened and more confident in their broadened perception of the world.

I got positive feedback from the participants who took part in the simulation. When asked whether they thought the virtual Minecraft world was useful, they replied with a variety of comments, including:

I think it would be. The simulation would be useful for people getting ready to go to Japan because they can learn various aspects such as train systems.

It gets the students thinking, like, oh, I should take off my shoes, or I should bow. Just little things like that to get them in the mindset of learning and understanding those different aspects of culture.

> *The virtual world was so fun and helpful for Americans because they could imagine the scene. In addition, there was so much information about Japan such as Sakura [cherry blossom], escalator etiquette, and so on. People can learn about Japan.*

The simulation's ultimate purpose was to teach the participants to be more receptive to a foreign culture and to be aware of the emotional challenges in doing so, and I hope it was achieved.

The Missing Piece

In my mind, a lot of the world's problems come down to a battle between the collective and the individual. While some want to move forward as a group, others believe that rising up and standing strong on an issue as an individual is the right path. Sometimes, however, those who protect their individualist ideals in what they believe to be correct can do so to the detriment of their wider community. It's complicated balancing an individual's freedom of choice with what is best for the greater good.

In many situations in my life, I've had to consider the greater good just to survive. Had I grown up in America, there's a good chance my interaction with Asian people would have gone no further than Dr Chen, and with my limited understanding, I might have bullied or humiliated others. Equally, I could just as likely have become fascinated with Japanese culture without fully understanding it, and could have filled my bookshelves with Japanese *manga* [comics] written in English. I may still have enjoyed eating sushi, identified with *anime* characters from Japanese video and film, and even taken Japanese language lessons – but would I have still gotten close to Japanese people in my personal relationships?

The point I am trying to make here is that cultural appreciation and cultural appropriation are quite the opposite. Appreciation is when someone seeks to understand and learn about another culture in an effort to broaden their perspective or connect with others cross-culturally. Cultural appropriation, in contrast, is when someone seeks personal attention or self-satisfaction by inappropriately adopting a feature of a culture that is not their own, especially something of important cultural significance. Here are two statements from an article on *The Insider* website that I think define the terms clearly: "If you show love and appreciation for parts of a culture, such as clothing, hairstyles, or accessories, but remain prejudiced against its people, that's appropriation." And: "On the other hand, if you learn, explore, and understand a different culture and then show that in a style that you've developed over time, that's appreciation."[10]

There's a fine line between appreciating a culture and appropriating it. Disney's popular film *Moana* is an example that drew criticism from scholars and Polynesians alike. Although the voyaging story is educational and adventurous, the heroic character of Maui was offensive to some Polynesians as he fulfills negative stereotypes of obesity and ignorance. Another example related to Polynesians is the cultivation of *kalo* [taro]. Were Wade to grow this Polynesian staple plant with its rich cultural importance purely for the sake of landscaping aesthetic, he would be trespassing on Hawaiian culture or using it for his personal gratification. However, because he nurtures the plants for consumption and prepares traditional dishes like luau stew or laulau, he is both acknowledging and respecting this plant's importance to Polynesian culture. Likewise, when I represented my Indiana high school by wearing a Japanese men's *yukata*, a lightweight cotton kimono, I was demonstrating the pride I have in my Japanese culture. It was my way of honoring Japan, not to seek attention.

Although I've accepted my destiny, I still feel I am seeking the final piece of the puzzle. It's something the Japanese call *ikigai*, or one's reason for being. The concept of *ikigai* can be explained as finding one's personal intersection point when the following four areas converge: mission (global urgency and destiny), passion (love and talent), vocation (calling), and profession (employment). Recently I've been co-teaching a seminar on peace studies. My colleague, Mika, and I developed the course to introduce the concepts of peace and conflict resolution through the study of historical and current affairs. Each week over Zoom, Mika and I prepare and present concepts and examples to a class of around 20 students. One student from a class said her idea of peace is that men and women are equal in society. Another said he learned peace building and cooperation by working within a group. One comment in particular pleased me: "From this class, I learned about the idea of peace in its various forms and how to create it."

Writing my own 3D journey through the stages of culture shock has made me more aware of the identity struggles I suffered growing up. I'm lucky to have emerged as a guide for others at the start of their intercultural journey. However, standing on the precipice of another significant change in my life – relocation to Japan – I am wondering, *Why am I drawn back to Japan?* I have no idea where my path will lead in Tokyo, but even as an expat living in Japan, I hope to continue contributing to cross-cultural understanding by bridging Eastern and Western cultures in any way I can. In many ways, I am a chip off the old block: Dad's influence in my life is evident as I face my own entrepreneurial challenges. Now in Japan, I am confident and prepared to go back through the stages of culture shock as an adult. I trust in the process; I know it will be worth it.

NOTES

1   Reflecting on my own experience, I better understood how it may have been difficult for Dad to overcome culture shock (Stage 2) while living in Japan. Dad had been an ice hockey player in his younger days and was competitive in sports. His mom, Martha, or GrandMarty as I called her, was a classy lady who always welcomed me with open arms. Going to her house was like traveling to a palace, where I had to behave around the collection of *objets d'art* throughout her fashionable home. GrandMarty was a beautiful lady, always well-coiffed, and on any given day took as meticulous care of her appearance as she did her home. My dad was her only son

and youngest child. He had three older sisters, my Aunt Kass, Aunt Patty, and Aunt Jean.

2   *Country comparison.* (n.d.). Hofstede insights. Retrieved July 28, 2021, from https://www.hofstede-insights.com/country-comparison/the-usa/

3   A good example of this is the desk I used to write this book. I decided to save up and get one of those height-adjustable desks, the kind with a motor that can extend the legs. Although I could have gotten a cheaper desk, the decision to buy this one has served me well.

4   Researchers have found that Japanese children learn in school to fix their eyes on their teacher's neck area. As adults, they naturally lower their gaze when conversing with their superiors as a sign of respect. Moran, R. T., Harris, P. R., & Moran, S. V. (2011). *Managing cultural differences: Global leadership strategies for the 21st century* (7th ed., pp. 40-74). Butterworth-Heinemann-Elsevier.

5   Bales, C. (2018, October 1). *09-08-18 Music video.* YouTube. https://www.youtube.com/watch?v=Eea_zmiaUEw

6   A Japanese phenomenon, *shikishi* are often used for special occasions and illustrate personal messages of farewell, appreciation, and sometimes poetry. Commonly given in school or work settings, these cardboard message boards are meant to be displayed and remembered. Although there is no equivalent in American culture, school yearbooks might be the closest similarity.

7   King Kamehameha I, or Kamehameha the Great, was from the Big Island and is known as the founder and first ruler of the Kingdom of Hawai'i. Among his many great deeds, through hard-fought battles and negotiations, he conquered and unified all of the islands into one kingdom. The Kalanikūpule were the opposing forces from the island of O'ahu.

8   *Equity vs. equality: What's the difference?* (2020, November 5). Milken Institute School of Public Health at The George Washington University. Retrieved July 5, 2021, from https://onlinepublichealth.gwu.edu/resources/equity-vs-equality/

9   The Japan Broadcasting Corporation (NHK) reported in May 2019 that antisocial behavior had become a national problem.
Eiraku, M. (2019, May 5). *Japan's 'Hikikomori' are growing older.* NHK World-Japan. https://www3.nhk.or.jp/nhkworld/en/news/backstories/464/

10   Dodgson, L. (2020, September 4). *People of color explain the difference between cultural appropriation and appreciation.* Insider. https://www.insider.com/difference-between-cultural-appropriation-and-appreciation-2020-9

QR code for
Chapter Seven
photographs

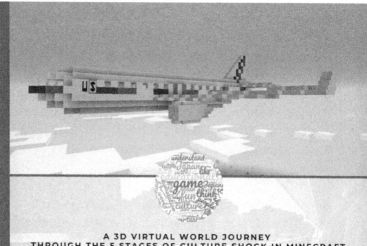

A 3D VIRTUAL WORLD JOURNEY
THROUGH THE 5 STAGES OF CULTURE SHOCK IN MINECRAFT

Embark on an adventure through an instructional simulation as a college student

preparing to study abroad in Japan. The virtual world learning environment (VWLE)

begins in a suburban American town where the participant arrives in Tokyo and

then travels to a suburban Japanese town that borders the countryside.

HTTPS://WWW.PLANETMINECRAFT.COM/PROJECT/
5-STAGES-OF-CULTURE-SHOCK/

'BECOMING' AMID PANDEMIC EXTREMISM (2021-2022)

Lingering Uneasiness

"Have you finished writing your memoirs?" Yuki asked me as we once again began our usual daily walk just before dusk.

The Hawaiian sun was slowly beginning to set in the west as we looked over the expansive sea below. Indeed, we lived in the middle of the Pacific Ocean, on the most isolated chain of islands on earth. Inside, however, my thoughts were whirring far across the sea. I felt uncomfortable. I was thinking of how our society, a racist society built by white men like me, had chosen to exclude so many others.

"I've shared the important memories, but I'm still tweaking things here and there. Oh, Bun," I said, calling her by a nickname, "we've been cooped up for months now in our small apartment. Writing has got me thinking about the past, present, and our upcoming relocation to Japan." I was half lost in thought as I stared into the distance.

What will the future hold? I wondered as a passing rain shower pushed us under our umbrella for a cuddle for the remainder of our stroll. I thought of how anti-Asian hate crimes had doubled since I wrote the introduction to this book. *Moving to Japan might be in Yuki's best interest.* In the meantime, we were preparing for that trip to Indiana. I really wanted my family there to meet her before we left the country.

We had both been fully vaccinated through our employer, but the attitude of some Americans toward being vaccinated and wearing masks was still unreasonable and self-centered, displaying a flagrant disregard for others. *How do you know who has or hasn't received a vaccine? Why are there so many unwilling to get a vaccine in America when people in other countries are so anxious to receive one?* Americans were now being coaxed to get vaccines in some states with promises of cash, gift cards, trips, and even Super Bowl tickets. Some companies and some government entities were taking things further by mandating vaccines. Showing a vaccine card to eat in my favorite restaurants was becoming commonplace.

Back then, only 29% of the Japanese population had been vaccinated. Cases were on the rise, with the Tokyo Olympic Games enveloped in controversy, and a majority of Japanese wanted the games to be cancelled (again) or postponed. After all, Tokyo was in another State of Emergency with the Delta variant surging. *Does Japan want to save face on the world stage?* I wasn't surprised, however, that the Olympics went ahead anyway. With Japan ranking on Hofstede's 6 Dimensions Model of National Cultures as one of the most uncertainty avoidance countries on the planet (92 out of 100),[1] Tokyo was more prepared than other cities for the unknown. Life there was highly ritualized. The Japanese were experts at prescribing maximum predictability and calculating unforeseen variables. Every possible scenario was considered which, in my mind, prepared them to be the perfect host. I believe that, considering the pandemic, had the Olympics been held in another country, the games would not have been as successful. Whether it was right or wrong to hold the games, Tokyo may have been the ideal city to host them, despite the fervent protests of its citizens.

My 2020 Virtual Graduation

Rather than the 2020 graduation ceremony my fellow master's students and I had envisioned, we were treated to a virtual graduation complete with the national anthem, university theme song, and speeches. I was the first name called by our Department Chairman to the Hawaiian foliage-adorned stage, emerging as an avatar character from among my classmates in Diamond Head Amphitheatre.[2] My pre-submitted comments thanking family, friends, and faculty for their support were read by one of my professors as I was virtually lei-d with a floating flower necklace. In Hawai'i, it's common to receive a lei (a wreath or garland worn around the neck) to celebrate a graduation. Friends and family the world over tuned in to the 5:00 pm Hawai'i Standard Time (HST) live-streamed video.

More surprising was my selection as one of three nominees for the department's Burniske Award for best thesis project: a distinct honor, even if I didn't win.

Creative measures are needed when common things are unavailable and life is shut down. Abnormalities demand improvisation and imagination. That virtual graduation was celebrated by a mock, social-distancing-approved live restaurant venue at Mom and Wade's home. They turned part of their yard into a new culinary establishment – the Kulakoa Coconut Café – where my wife and I were quarantined to a table for two with a 5-course menu printed on cardstock next to pink heart-shaped cloth napkins left over from our wedding reception. Greeted with fragrant genuine flower leis, tropical cocktails, and congratulations galore, we were elated at the attention. It turned out to be a graduation celebration that was perhaps more memorable than usual – in spite of the restrictions.

Positive Initiatives

In December 2020, I attended a special online event presented by Families in Global Transition (FIGT), the same organization where I had been a guest panelist years before at the age of 14. *Third Culture Kids & Parachute Kids: Building their Resilience* was the topic and naturally interesting to me, especially in light of the current pandemic. I was particularly impressed by the research of Dr Tim Stuart, an adult TCK of mixed race and co-author of *Children At Promise*. Dr Stuart mentioned how adversity plays an important role in how TCKs progress from resilience to rejuvenation. His research has studied 13 variables attributable to successful TCKs, two of which he finds as most significant. First, did the TCK have an adult who cared about them? Second, did the TCK have a belief system that correlated with their ability to accept diversity?[3] Reflecting back on my own experience of 'mixed blessings,' I am happy to be able to respond affirmatively to those two questions. In their co-authored book, Dr Stuart and his colleague present their scientific study on how both at-risk and advantaged children can realize their 'At Promise' identity.

I continue to don a mask these days to enter a crowded space, a public building, or public transportation because I feel connected to the wider global response, unable to forget how we're in this together. I find the phrase 'we're in this together' almost synonymous with the response to the pandemic. With the release of three vaccines from Pfizer, Moderna, and Johnson & Johnson, the American public now has a lifeline to protect itself. The Biden Administration has also promised to speed up the distribution of vaccinations in order to reach a level of herd immunity and to become an arsenal for the distribution of vaccines to other countries in an effort to combat the virus globally.[4]

On January 26, 2021, President Biden signed an Executive Order addressing the xenophobia and "skyrocketing hate crimes" perpetrated in recent months toward Asian Americans and Pacific Islanders.[5] Later, on May 20, 2021, the Hate Crimes Act was signed into law aiming to address the surge in attacks on Asian Americans amid the COVID-19 pandemic. It's a relief that this issue has been acknowledged at the highest level.

Same Storm, Different Boats

The information highway of the Internet is today's source of seeking self-enlightenment. As the Internet continues to evolve into what many call the 'metaverse,' the reality of transitioning into virtual environments may soon become the norm. As new COVID variants emerge that nullify current vaccines, I wonder if this might push society further in the direction of the metaverse as our new way of life? The Internet is a tremendous communicative tool for teaching global literacy and helping people to make sense of cultures when they collide. Signs, billboards, books, advertisements, newspapers, magazines, and digital platforms provide each person with knowledge. Everyday words surround us as published writing or 'media speak' that tempt, warn or call us either toward global literacy or back into our boxing corners. Though dismantling fake news and disarming political conflict might be a job for others, it's every person's responsibility to navigate through truth and falsehood among these messages. The acquisition of knowledge is a personal journey.

I recently heard a good analogy for our current situation: "We are all in the same storm, but in different boats." Collective humanity is impossible without accepting each other's differences. When cultures and people collide, and they will, it should be our purpose to survive our shock or outrage, bridge our divides, understand our differences, patch up our conflicts, repair our damage, and figure out our common goal. Biologically, race is not real. It's a social construct that comes from subconscious programming and misunderstanding. If I have learned anything from my TCK experience, it is this: anyone is capable of developing tolerance, celebrating diversity, and manifesting acceptance toward others. Inclusion is not a head issue; it's a heart issue. To accept those who are different is a choice.

NOTES

1   *Country comparison.* (n.d.). Hofstede insights. Retrieved July 29, 2021, from https://www.hofstede-insights.com/country-comparison/japan/

2   UHM Learning Design and Technology. (2020, May 8). LTEC virtual graduation 2020 [video]. Facebook. https://www.facebook.com/362971297113240/videos/1082717318759566

3   Stuart, T. S., & Bostrom, C. G. (2005). *Children at promise: 9 principles to help kids thrive in an at risk world.* Wiley.

4   Collins, K., & Sullivan, K. (2021, May 17). *Biden announces US will share more vaccines globally: 'Our nation is going to be the arsenal of vaccines'.* CNN. https://www.cnn.com/2021/05/17/politics/vaccines-global-sharing-biden-administration/index.html

5   Briefing Room. (2021, January 26). Memorandum condemning and combating racism, xenophobia, and intolerance against Asian Americans and Pacific Islanders in the United States. The White House.

https://www.whitehouse.gov/briefing-room/presidential-actions/2021/01/26/memorandum-condemning-and-combating-racism-xenophobia-and-intolerance-against-asian-americans-and-pacific-islanders-in-the-united-states/

GLOSSARY OF JAPANESE AND FOREIGN WORDS/TERMS

Note: many definitions are cross-referenced with *jisho.org*

A

ame to muchi – candy and whip; meaning reward and punishment
anime – Japanese cartoons; animated films or cartoons

B

beni imo – Okinawan purple sweet potato
boku – pronoun meaning I or me, most commonly used by males
butsudan – household altar; commonly used to commune with ancestors

C

chan – an affectionate suffix most commonly used for a daughter, girl, or close friend
Chuo-sen – one of the primary train lines in the greater Tokyo area that has the orange color

D

Daibutsu – large statue of Buddha; most often used to refer to the giant Buddha statues in Kamamura and Nara
dangomushi – pillbug; pill bug, slater, crustacean that rolls into a ball; roly-poly

deru kui ha utareru – a phrase meaning the nail that sticks up gets pounded into place

deshita – past tense form of *desu*, which means 'to be'

dō – path or way; method

E

F

futon – traditional Japanese bedding consisting of a mattress and a duvet

G

gaijin – slang for foreigner; outsider; stranger

gaikokujin – foreigner; outsider

gakuran – school uniform for boys

gaman – Japanese concept or term commonly translated as perseverance, patience, or tolerance

ganbatte – an expression of encouragement to mean 'you can do it'

genkan – entryway of a house

geta – Japanese wooden clogs

gochisosama – phrase to express 'thank you for the meal' or 'that was a delicious meal'

gomennasai – formal expression of apology; I'm sorry; my apologies; excuse me

gomi – trash; garbage

Gōng Shǐ Fā Tsaí – Happy Lunar New Year; or more literally, wishing someone prosperity in the coming year

gōya – bitter melon

H

hanafuda – traditional Japanese playing cards

haole – Hawaiian slang word for foreigners but particularly in reference to white people; literally, the word *hā ʻole* means 'without breath' as the first visitors to the islands had no knowledge of the Hawaiian customary greeting of touching nose to nose and sharing each other's breaths

happi – traditional Japanese straight-sleeved short coat

hayaku – an expression meaning 'hurry up'

hikikomori – a person who has withdrawn from society; social withdrawal

hiragana – cursive Japanese syllabary used primarily for native Japanese words

hon – book

I

ikigai – one's purpose and reason for living; or the French phrase *raison d'être*

iro uchikake – a woman's traditional and colorful bridal robe

itadakimasu – phrase to express 'thank you for the meal (just served)' or 'I will receive this meal'

J

jankenpon – rock! scissors! paper! hand game

jidensha – bicycle or literally translated as self (*ji*) train (*densha*)

K

Kaigai Shijo Kyoiku – Japan Overseas Educational Services Publication

kalo – Hawaiian taro plant

kamemushi – stink bug

kami – paper

kanji – Chinese written characters

kara – empty; emptiness; open; blank

karate – empty hand; martial art

karōshi – death by overwork

katakana – angular Japanese syllabary used primarily for loan or foreign words

ki – inner energy commonly associated with martial arts; also known as *qi* in Chinese

kimchi – spicy Korean pickled cabbage

kimono – traditional Japanese T-shaped garment

Kodomo no hi – Translated as Children's Day, this holiday is celebrated on May 5 each year

koi – carp

kokugo – Japanese national language; school subject

koshihikari – variety of rice developed in Fukui prefecture; now also grown in Australia and the United States

kowa – an abbreviated version of the Japanese word *kowai*, which means scary or frightening

kun – an affectionate suffix most commonly used for a boy, male, or close friend

kuni – country; state; region

L

lanai – Hawaiian word for patio of a home or condo; outdoor area

M

(high) maka maka – Hawaiian word meaning stuck up or pretentious; superior attitude

mamachari – traditional ladies' bicycle with a basket in front; often used for transporting children

mamushi – venomous pit viper

manga – Japanese comic book; cartoon drawings with dialogue *matsuri* – festival

meiwaku – to annoy or cause other person(s) trouble

menehune – mythical Hawaiian characters that resemble gnomes or dwarfs

mikan – mandarin orange; tangerine

mochi – Japanese pounded rice; (sticky) rice cake; usually eaten at the New Year and other special occasions

monozukuri – craftsmanship; manufacturing; making things by hand

montsuki haori hakama – Japanese traditional formal attire for men

N

nattō – fermented soybeans

negi – green onion; spring onion

nihonshu – Japanese rice wine made by polishing and fermenting rice

ninja – a person trained in *ninjutsu* and employed for covert purposes in feudal Japan

ninjutsu – martial art form used in combat and stealth techniques used by Japanese *ninja*, especially in assassination.

nisei – 2nd generation Japanese born outside of Japan

nishikigoi – the proper name for the colorful variety of Japanese brocaded carp

no – a particle indicating possession

O

o-bāchan – affectionate way to say grandma; elderly woman

obon – Buddhist festival of the dead held each year during August to pay respects to the deceased

ofuro – bath; bathing room in a home

okole – Hawaiian word for butt; backside

okonomi – choice; preference; whatever you like

okonomiyaki – a grilled savory pancake containing a variety of meat or seafood and vegetables; a grilled savory pancake filled with whatever you like

oni – Japanese word for devil or demon

oni wa soto! fuku wa uchi! – Japanese expression used on *Setsubun* meaning 'Devils out, happiness in'

onsen – hot spring; spa

P

pōpolo – Hawaiian slang word for dark-skinned or black people; the name of a nightshade plant that produces dark-colored berries

Q

R

ramen – Chinese-style noodles commonly served in various soup bases

ramune – traditional Japanese soft drink produced in a glass bottle with a marble stopper

randoseru – traditional leather backpack used by school children

S

sake – alcohol; any type of alcohol but most commonly associated with Japanese *nihonshu*

samurai – Japanese warrior; military retainer of feudal lords during the Edo period

sansei – 3rd generation Japanese born outside of Japan

sensei – used as a title to address a teacher, master, doctor, lawyer, or professional in their field

sentō – Japanese communal bathhouse; public bath
Setsubun – Japanese festival held one day before the start of spring based on the Japanese lunar calendar
shiki – mathematical formula
shinkansen – bullet train
shinnen akemashite omedetou gozaimasu – Happy New Year
sho – handwriting; writing
shodō – calligraphy
shōgakkō – elementary school
sōji – cleaning; sweeping; dusting; scrubbing
soju – Korean spirit typically distilled from rice or sweet potatoes
sumimasen – formal expression to say excuse me; pardon me; I'm sorry; I beg your pardon

T

tabi – Japanese traditional footwear
taiko – drum
Tanabata – Japanese star festival usually held on July 7th when children and adults write wishes on colorful strips of paper which are tied onto bamboo branches
tanuki – racoon dog
tatami – Japanese-style grass floor mats
te – hand
tofu – bean curd
tōyu – kerosene fuel

U

umaibō – Japanese puffed corn stick snack that comes in various flavors
unchi – poop
undokai – sports day; sports festival

uruwashii – Japanese word meaning beautiful; heartwarming; fair

W
watashi – slightly formal pronoun meaning I or me, most commonly used by females

Y
yaki – grilled cooking technique
yen – currency of Japan represented with the ¥ symbol
yōchien – kindergarten
yuimaru – the strong bonds supporting a community of people that regulate mind/body balance
yukata – light cotton *kimono* worn in the summer season or often used as a bathrobe at *onsens*
yuki – snow; snowfall
yukiguni – snow country; area that often receives heavy snowfall
Yukimi Daifuku – A Japanese brand of *mochi* ice cream

Z
zōkin – rag commonly used to clean the floor; dust cloth

SUGGESTED FURTHER READING

Barnes, B. E. (2006). *Culture, Conflict, and Mediation in the Asian Pacific.* University Press of America.

Eakin, K. B. (1998). *According to my Passport, I'm Coming Home.* Department of State: Family Liaison Office.

Hofstede, G., Hofstede, G. J., & Minkov, M. (2010). *Cultures and Organizations: Software of the Mind.* (3rd ed.). McGraw Hill.

Moran, R. T., Harris, P. R., & Moran, S. V. (2011). *Managing cultural differences: Global leadership strategies for the 21st century* (7th ed., pp. 40-74). Butterworth-Heinemann-Elsevier.

Obama, B. (2004). *Dreams from my Father: A Story of Race and Inheritance.* Three Rivers Press.

Oberg, K. (1960). Cultural Shock: Adjustment to New Cultural Environments. *Practical Anthropology*, (4), 177-182. https://doi.org/10.1177/009182966000700405

Ota, D. W. (2014). *Safe Passage: How Mobility Affects People & What International Schools Should Do about It.* Summertime Publishing.

O'Shaughnessy, C. (2014). *Arrivals, Departures and the Adventures In-Between.* Summertime Publishing.

Pollock, D. C., & Van Reken, R. E. (1999). *The Third Culture Kid Experience: Growing Up Among Worlds.* Nicholas Brealey Publishing.

Pollock, D. C., & Van Reken, R. E. (2001). *Third Culture Kids: The Experience of Growing Up Among Worlds.* Nicholas Brealey Publishing.

Quick, T. (2010). *The Global Nomad's Guide to University Transition.* Summertime Publishing.

Stuart, T. S., & Bostrom, C. G. (2005). *Children At Promise: 9 Principles to Help Kids Thrive in an At-Risk World.* Wiley.

ABOUT THE AUTHOR

Casey Eugene Bales, otherwise known as '*Keeshi-kun*,' lives his destiny as a bridge between America and Japan. He spent ten of his formative years being schooled in the Japanese educational system in Japan. Later, he attended Japanese school in the United States, thereby completing his entire K-12 education as the only  non-Japanese in each grade level. From 2001 thru 2005, he earned High School diplomas from both the United States and Japan. Aside from writing his memoirs, he thrives on bringing people together, challenging existing attitudes, and fostering cultural consciousness. He worked at Hawaii Tokai International College from 2013 to 2022 and holds a BBA Degree in International Business and Finance and an M.Ed. Degree in Instructional Design and Technology. Having grown up as a Third Culture Kid (TCK), Casey is continuing his cultural journey in Tokyo, Japan, with his wife, Yuki. His leisure activities include videography, online activities, and social encounters with friends. "This is the way" is his all-time favorite quote.

If you'd like to learn more or connect with Casey, please reach out to him through the methods below.

 www.caseybales.com

 www.linkedin.com/in/caseybales/

Also from **Summertime Publishing**

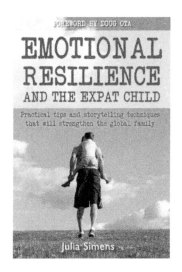

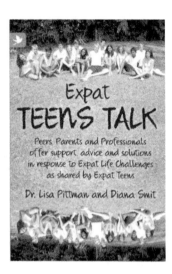

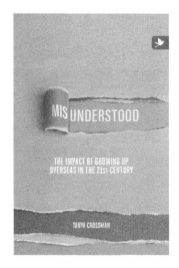

Printed in Great Britain
by Amazon